The Gosp

MW01169845

"... I found this book to be engaging, informative, challenging, and convicting ... "
— **Russell Moore, *Christianity Today***

" ... I'm so grateful for this helpful work from Tyler Zach ... Recommend!"
— **Scott Sauls, senior pastor of Christ Presbyterian Church and author of *Jesus Outside the Lines* and *A Gentle Answer***

" ... *The Gospel for Individualists* not only is an incredible tool for me but it has also helped my family and my friends understand me better. I believe there is no greater gift than loving God, loving others, and loving yourself...this devotional helps me pursue all three."
— **Ben Higgins, from ABCs hit show *The Bachelor***

" ... On these pages, Tyler's creative wisdom shines, and his focus always remains on Jesus ... "
— **Beth & Jeff McCord, co-founders of Your Enneagram Coach, best-selling authors of *Becoming Us: Using the Enneagram to Create a Thriving Gospel-Centered Marriage***

" ... an extraordinary gift to all Enneagram enthusiasts ... "
— **Marilyn Vancil, author of *Self to Lose, Self to Find: Using the Enneagram to Uncover Your True, God-Gifted Self***

" ... Through a tapestry of Scripture, quotes, and metaphors, Tyler tenderly guides Fours back to the truth of who we were made to be ... I feel more alive reading, writing, and reflecting thanks to this gift of a book!"
— **Meredith McDaniel, Licensed Clinical Mental Health Counselor and author of *In Want + Plenty***

The Gospel for Individualists

A 40-Day Devotional for Passionate, Unique Creatives

BY TYLER ZACH

The Gospel for Individualists: A 40-Day Devotional for Passionate, Unique Creatives: (Enneagram Type 4)

© 2021 by Tyler Zach

Edited by Joshua Casey, Stephanie Cross, and Lee Ann Roberts

Scripture quotations are from the ESV® Bible (The Holy Bible, English Standard Version®), copyright © 2001 by Crossway, a publishing ministry of Good News Publishers. Used by permission. All rights reserved.

Cover design by Fruitful Design (www.fruitful.design)
Interior Design and eBook by Kelley Creative (www.kelleycreative.design)

ISBN: 9798515829964

www.gospelforenneagram.com

To Lindsey, my wonderful bride, who is radiantly beautiful, fiercely loyal, enduringly faithful, and the greatest encourager in my life.

Table of Contents

Foreword

WHEN JEFF AND I FIRST DISCOVERED THE Enneagram, it wasn't easy finding books written from a Christian worldview. We understood how important gospel-centered Enneagram resources could be, and that inspired us to start our business, Your Enneagram Coach. Since then, we've helped over 1,500,000 people find their Type through our free assessment, and grow through our online classes, coaching certifications, books, and now a podcast.

I'm so thankful you've picked up this devotional because that means you've decided to invest in yourself. I believe you will feel understood for the first time on a level deeper than any person has understood you before. I pray that this will be a glimpse of the reality of how much your Heavenly Father knows you, understands you, and cherishes you as you are. He created you to be an introspective individualist who is unique and special. He delights in who you are and comes close to you in every way.

The Enneagram is a tool that clarifies our fallen nature while also reminding us we are created in the *imago Dei* (image of God). When Jeff and I understood the why behind our thoughts and actions, it transformed how we looked at ourselves, our relationship with God, our marriage, our parenting, and (obviously) our careers. Taking a risk by starting a business was both exciting and terrifying. We could have easily spun out of control or run out of gas (at times we did!), but seeing the Enneagram through the lens of the gospel kept us grounded and on track.

The world needs Type Fours. You see the profound despair and suffering in the world and bravely press into those depths to discover rich meaning in all of life. You embrace a wide range of emotions and experiences, bringing a unique beauty, depth, creativity, and understanding to any event or situation.

Just as you are eager to explore the depths of our complicated world in a search for meaning and authentic connections, you desire to look inside yourself to find your unique significance and value. However, when you do, a constant feeling burdens you that you are missing something important and that you're flawed in ways no one else is. Craving ideal circumstances or love, you often cannot stop pondering what is missing in your life and exploring your sense of disconnectedness.

Struggling with feelings of envy, you compare yourself to others, longing for what you don't have while believing others have what you long to possess. However, when you take the longings of your heart to Christ and step out from under the waterfall of your emotions, you bring forth your talents in ways that are truly extraordinary. You have a deep intuition of how others feel when they are suffering and can listen to people's pains and deep emotions; they don't overwhelm you. In fact, connecting with others on a deep level and being there for them in their pain brings you great joy, which is an amazing gift to the world.

Jeff and I are thankful the Lord has provided more gospel-centered Enneagram teachers like Tyler Zach. Whether you are new to the Enneagram or have studied it for years, we know that you'll find lasting value in this book. On these pages, Tyler's creative wisdom shines, and his focus always remains on Jesus. We're praying that God will meet you on these pages, and you will recognize your inherent value as His beloved child.

Jesus is the author and perfecter of our faith (Hebrews 12:2). He finished the great task He set out to do (John 19:30). A vital part of His ministry was to stay in alignment with His Father, and He did this by setting aside time for rest and reflection. He invites you to do the same—to come away, separate from the crowds, and BE with Him. Remember, you are loved and valued for simply being you. You do not have to be different or unique to gain Christ's approval. You are loved and seen right now as you are.

—**Beth and Jeff McCord**
co-founders of Your Enneagram Coach
best-selling authors of *Becoming Us: Using the Enneagram to Create a Thriving Gospel-Centered Marriage*

Introduction:

The Gospel for Individualists

THERE'S NO ONE LIKE *YOU*. YOU ARE a unique, one-of-a-kind, gift from the Divine Artist to the world. You are an old soul with the innovative heart of a groundbreaking artist, likely spending your life feeling as though you were born both too late and way too soon. When at your best, time with you can be like sitting in an old church building, secure in its strong foundation and towering place in the world. Sitting in the silent holiness—timeworn pews holding vigil, the sun's strong, gentle rays reaching out to us through a myriad of bright panes in tall stained-glass windows—allows us to feel both securely known and inspired.

Make no mistake: though this book is wrapped in only one color, the truth is that Enneagram Fours (who I'll also refer to as Individualists) come in an infinite variety of shades and hues. The inspiration for this book's dark violet color comes from German poet and philosopher Johann Wolfgang von Goethe (1749–1832) who shared that "Violet is both a symbol of the highest rapture of the soul ... as well as of its darkest and most painful moments. ... In its oscillations passion comes into contact with intoxication, liberation with decay, death with resurrection, pain with redemption, disease with purification, mystical vision with madness."[1]

Goethe's description only begins to describe the mysterious, otherworldly, multilayered, deeply intriguing, living paradox that is *you*. I'll never be able to fully understand you and I'm okay with that; there is, after all, no true beauty without mystery. You are to us an iconic symbol whose life and work transcends language, space, and time—which is why the world keeps coming back to you for more.

---

1   Richard Rohr and Andreas Ebert, *The Enneagram: A Christian Perspective* (Crossroad Pub, 2001), 108.

Over the next 40 days, I want to come alongside you to muse on profound insights together, navigate both the pain and pleasures of life, point you to the God who understands you perfectly, and persuade you of all the wonderful qualities you possess. I also want to help you turn your creative passion into action, bring balance to your inner-world and relationships, teach you how to survive the real world while living outside the box, and demonstrate how to chanel all of the beauty and suffering you've experienced so that you can engage the whole world with the wholeness of Christ.

Trust me, I don't have all the answers. But I promise that by the end, you'll be able to see yourself a little clearer and hopefully see why God is so crazy about you. Because Fours are said to be the least common personality type (and most misunderstood), my deepest desire is to encourage you fully. I truly believe God will use the words on these pages to persuade you that God can't love you any more or any less—although I know it's a daily battle to believe that truth sometimes. In Him, you have someone who is present with you, bears witness to your pain, and grieves with you in the struggle.

The Enneagram can be a helpful and necessary part of spiritual growth through self-awareness. Unlike other "personality" profiles, the aim of the Enneagram is to uncover why we do what we do—to help us see what lies behind our strengths and weaknesses. If we use this as a diagnostic tool and allow the Bible to provide the language for our interpretation, then the Enneagram can produce great change in our lives, relationships, and work.

This is a book about Enneagram types, but don't be mistaken. Fundamentally, I'm a pastor who believes the Bible is the inspired Word of God and is sufficient for all He requires us to believe and do. That said, I *also* believe God has provided additional insights in fields, such as medicine and psychology, that are helpful in understanding the incredible world God has made. We must tread carefully as we draw insights from fields with limited horizons of evidence like psychology. (We still have so much more to learn about the brain!) As with any anything we come across in this fallible world, we can put on our gospel lens and make use of the wisdom God has poured out on the whole human race.

So What Makes This Book Different?

While there are other projects explaining the Enneagram, the primary aim of this book is to go deeper by applying the truth of God's Word specifically to your type over the next 40 days. If you are suspicious of the Enneagram or know someone who is, download my free resource called "Should Christians Use The Enneagram?" at gospelforenneagram.com. I pray it will help you engage with the Enneagram as a Christian, and then talk about it with others.

Before we get to the daily devotions, let's look at how the gospel both affirms and challenges the unique characteristics of your type.

The Gospel Affirms Individualists

God sympathizes with the worldview of an Individualist. This inauthentic and insensitive world lacks depth and is filled with predictable, superficial, trendy, and tacky people. We need intuitive and imaginative leaders who will show the hurting empathy, add beauty to every area of our lives, express the inexpressible, teach us about our humanity, and share with us the many wonders and mysteries of this life. Therefore, an Individualist will be happy to know that the Bible affirms the following beliefs:

• **God created us all unique.** "For you formed my inward parts; you knitted me together in my mother's womb. I praise you, for I am fearfully and wonderfully made. Wonderful are your works; my soul knows it very well."[2]

• **God created us as deeply sensitive beings.** "Be kind to one another, tenderhearted, forgiving one another, as God in Christ forgave you."[3]

• **God created us to live authentically**. "My frame was not hidden from you, when I was being made in secret, intricately woven in the depths of the earth."[4]

• **God created us to embrace joy *and* suffering**. "[Jesus] was despised and rejected by men, a man of sorrows and acquainted with grief; and as one from whom men hide their faces he was despised, and we esteemed him not."[5]

---

2   Ps. 139:13-14

3   Eph. 4:32

4   Ps. 139:15

5   Isa. 53:3

- **God created us to care about the aesthetics.** "The Lord said to Moses, 'See, I have called by name Bezalel the son of Uri, son of Hur, of the tribe of Judah, and I have filled him with the Spirit of God, with ability and intelligence, with knowledge and all craftsmanship, to devise artistic designs, to work in gold, silver, and bronze, in cutting stones for setting, and in carving wood, to work in every craft."[6]

- **God created the *whole* world: there is no difference between "sacred" and "secular."** "For everything created by God is good, and nothing is to be rejected if it is received with thanksgiving, for it is made holy by the word of God and prayer."[7]

- **God created us to fight for the underdog.** "Learn to do good; seek justice, correct oppression; bring justice to the fatherless, plead the widow's cause."[8]

- **God created us to long for eternity.** "And not only the creation, but we ourselves, who have the firstfruits of the Spirit, groan inwardly as we wait eagerly for adoption as sons, the redemption of our bodies."[9]

The Gospel Challenges Individualists

The gospel also provides specific challenges to Individualists. Now we'll explore the most common lies Individualists believe and see how the Bible provides much better promises and blessings. We will move more deeply into each of these throughout the course of the next 40 days.

- **Lie #1: I am deeply flawed.** One of the core fears of an Individualist is feeling *inadequate or flawed.* The best things about themselves are often "hidden in plain sight." I'm here to remind you that you are not some product that must be recalled because of manufacturer defects. You were woven together in your mother's womb by the Divine Artist. You are "very good"—complete. You are more loved and accepted in Jesus Christ than you ever dreamed. What is needed to combat negative self-esteem isn't a higher view of yourself, but rather an accurate view of yourself hidden in the love of Christ.

---

6   Ex. 31:1-5

7   1 Tim. 4:4–5

8   Isa. 1:17

9   Rom. 8:23

- **Lie #2: Something is missing.** The Individualist is on a never-ending search for their *missing piece*—which may lead to driving around endlessly in a cul-de-sac of introspection. Thus, *longing* becomes the Four's most intimate, lifelong companion and *envy* (that someone else surely has the missing piece) becomes the vice or core weakness. The good news is that Christ has not given more of Himself to others than He has to you. The truth is that you don't need more from the world, but that the world needs more of you. Rather than rooting your identity in one long search for completion, search for what's already within you: Christ, the hope of glory. In Christ, you have all you need to be worthy of love.

- **Lie #3: I will be abandoned.** Another core fear for the Individualist is coming off to others as either *too inadequate* or *too much* resulting in being emotionally cut off. Like Adam and Eve, Fours feel as if they've been expelled from their "lost paradise." Their deeply felt inner-experience is saturated by feelings of separation and loneliness. The good news is that God's drama centers around a Rescuer from heaven who comes to sweep us back into His waiting arms. You can bring every emotion to Him without fear of getting rejected. Your emotions aren't too much for Him. He loves you for who you are, not for who others want you to be. You are the one Christ lived and died for, and with Him you never have to be someone else.

- **Lie #4: No one will ever understand me.** It's true that you are deeply intriguing, always wrestling with paradoxes and living comfortably in the mysteries that most people avoid. Very few people will ever fully understand you and how you see the world. The truth is God understands us better than we understand ourselves. Our Creator is far more complex than we are; we are not a mystery to Him. Furthermore, Jesus Himself was misunderstood: the lamenting Man of Sorrows and innocent Suffering Servant—who chose pain over prosperity, who made us whole by His wounds, who absorbed darkness and transformed it into light—knows exactly what you are going through.

- **Lie #5: I am my feelings.** Jesus was a kaleidoscope of emotions, able to express the entire spectrum of human warmth and love, anger and frustration, grief and loss. But for you, *feelings* can quickly transpose your life from a healthy drama into a melodrama when they become a controlling, all-consuming, even enslaving force. When your identity is based upon a shifting thing like feelings, you will soon find your peace and self-worth swept away. But Jesus promises that those who build their house on the Rock—will live securely. As a child of God, you are no longer a slave but a steward of your emotions—to use for His redemptive purposes. *Equanimity*, the Four's virtue, literally means "an equal mind." When your mind is balanced, you can feel your feelings without becoming them and use them as a gauge rather than a guide.

- **Lie #6: I am loved for being unique and special.** You have been uniquely created to reflect the *imago Dei* by embodying the *originality* of God. But when you drift from the gospel's promise of unconditional love, you deteriorate into self-indulgence, working hard to project an image of unmatched uniqueness, drawing others' attention to your own unique style and works. Thus, the Four seeks to avoid being *ordinary* and getting stuck in the *mundane* activities of life. You must remember that blue-collar, Nazareth-born Jesus had no form, majesty, or beauty to be desired by the world[10]—and purposely chose ordinary men and women to turn the world upside down. Remember, the good news is that Jesus died on the cross for you—for your flawed and ordinary self, not your special, crafted self.

As you can see, the gospel will challenge your perception of the protagonists and antagonists in your life. In the Individualists's kingdom, those who make you feel extraordinary are rewarded. Your "heroes" become those who indulge your feelings, richly reward your abilities, and give you all the autonomy you want. Likewise, your "villains" become those who challenge you to think positively, call you to take action, ask you to put your feelings aside when the show must go on, or delegate mundane tasks that aren't any fun but still need to get done.

God's kingdom will not be filled with those who are special stand-outs in the eyes of the world, but rather ordinary men and women who called out for a Rescuer. In this place, self-absorption is exchanged for selflessness, envy is dispelled by contentment, and longing leads to belonging. In this place, daydreams become a reality, helplessness is replaced with individual responsibility, and people are able to express themselves fully without making it all about themselves. In this place, "you are no longer foreigners and strangers,"[11] but rather right at home in the household of God where nothing is missing.

---

10   Isa. 53:2

11   Eph. 2:19

The Invitation

When Jesus Christ, the Divine All in all, entered into flawed and limited human history, He started His mission with an invitation: "The time is fulfilled, and the kingdom of God is at hand; repent and believe in the gospel."[12] He explained that to enter the good, eternally renewing life that begins well before the grave, you must do two things: believe the truth and turn from sin. Believing includes acknowledging who God is, who He says we are, and what He has done for us. Turning includes shedding our false worldview, misplaced desires, strong defenses, hide-and-seek strategies, and self-salvation efforts.

If you are ready to begin this incredible 40-day journey and accept God's invitation, then let's go! It will be an enlightening ride of rapid growth in the days to come as you become more self-aware and experience newfound freedom. You will encounter many "aha" moments as you read profound truths for your type—and maybe even learn something about the people around you. The things you learn about yourself in this book will be guaranteed to stick with you for the rest of your life.

The Three Types of Individualists

Before we begin, I want to let you know that Fours can look vastly different from one another; so, before you dive into the daily devotions, you may want to check out the "Three Types of Individualists" in the back of this book. Though it's not necessary to have a firm grasp on these before proceeding, these subtypes are helpful in drilling down the different nuances of the Individualist and will explain why some truths in this devotional will hit home more than others. These descriptions tend to err on the negative side, but they are meant to help you further uncover the unconscious motivations driving your behavior and may even help you discover why you get confused with other Enneagram types!

---

12 Mark 1:15

Day 1:

Paradise Lost

Then the Lord God said, "Behold, the man has become like one of us in

knowing good and evil ..." therefore the Lord God sent him out from the garden

of Eden to work the ground from which he was taken. He drove out the man,

and at the east of the garden of Eden he placed the cherubim and a flaming

sword that turned every way to guard the way to the tree of life.

—Genesis 3:22-24

THE YOUNG MID-WESTERN GIRL FINDS HERSELF IN the eye of a storm. Too late to find refuge in the cellar, she holds her dog closely while the powerful cyclone carries them—girl, dog, and house—far, far away from their Kansas home.

The classic story, *The Wizard of Oz,* invites us to go with Dorthy along the yellow, brick road as she tries to find her way back home.

Of Man's First Disobedience, and the Fruit Of that Forbidden Tree, whose mortal taste Brought Death into the World, and all our woe.

–John Milton[1]

---

1 John Milton, *Paradise Lost: With Introd., Notes, and Diagrams* (United States: Ginn, 1886), XI.

Her fantastical journey is filled with memorable songs and unforgettable places; strange encounters with scarecrows, tin men, and lions lay along the path; singing munchkins, winged monkeys, witches (good and bad), and supposed wizards wait to offer advice, help, or waylay our heroes.

Dorthy's story is similar to ours. In the biblical account of humanity's first couple, Adam and Eve, were enjoying paradise, walking with God and experiencing the fullness of divinely intended joy, beauty, fruitfulness, and abundance. But when their enemy, the serpent, slithers into their lives, seeking to kill and destroy the love and trust between Creator and Creation. In an instant, the great doubt is introduced—that heartbreaking question: *Is this* really *all there is?* Feeling alone and abandoned, separated from God and the only home they had ever known—the place where they felt truly at peace—Adam and Eve are forced to relearn how to survive in an uncaring and unwelcoming world.

> What you are longing for right now, you already have in Christ.

Fours know the feeling well. Life feels like one long search, driven by an insatiable longing for "their lost paradise."[2] Their deeply felt inner experience is saturated by feelings of separation, loneliness, and lack of understanding. They simultaneously want to fit in with the rest of the world and dance along with everyone else but are driven by their own inner music, and as such always seem to be out of step with themselves and the world.

As a result, Fours perpetually mourn for the primordial connection they believe has been lost. Like a child peering in their own home's frosty window, watching their family open gifts on Christmas morning, there is an ever-present, gut-wrenching despair—a feeling of being left out, forgotten, and lost.

Being incredibly self-aware, it's not difficult for a Four to admit mankind's fault in severing the connection to God and His paradise. However, this knowledge of culpable lack leads many to believe these failures are fatal and final. Even worse, they believe this disconnect with peace and abundance to be the result of an inner deficiency—an insurmountable, inherent badness and inadequacy. They may

2 Jerome Wagner, *Nine Lenses on the World: The Enneagram Perspective* (NineLens Press, 2010), 271.

believe "there is something evil or poisonous about them" that is unredeemable and has caused God and others to abandon them permanently.[3] They think, "If God has abandoned me, then everyone else will too."

The Good News for Individualists is that this isn't the end of the story. God pulls back the curtain for the apostle John and gives him a symbolic vision of this world's final chapter in the Book of Revelation. In this vision, John sees the heavenly garden of Eden with the tree of life right in the middle, accessible to all and bearing satisfying, healing fruit.[4] People from every generation and ethnicity are there together, sharing this Divinely given abundance, knowing they belong with the same deep surety our first ancestors did in the garden.[5] In the end, those who felt like outsiders have now become insiders; those who once peered through the window with a feeling of abandonment, are now eating at the table of rich food and well-aged wine.[6]

At the end of Dorothy's story, she clicks her heels together three times, and says, "There's no place like home," then wakes up and realizes that she was home all the time![7] The same is true of you as a creation loved by the Creator. What you are longing for right now, you already have in Christ—the One who entered this world's story with all of its beauty and brokenness. God's drama centers around a Rescuer from heaven who comes to sweep us back into His waiting arms. From time to time, you maybe get swept up in the cyclone of emotions and feel far from home, but Jesus' promise remains the same: "I will never leave you nor forsake you."[8]

---

3   Sandra Maitri, *The Spiritual Dimension of the Enneagram: Nine Faces of the Soul* (United States: Penguin Publishing Group, 2000), 139.

4   Rev. 22:1-2

5   Rev. 7:9

6   Isa. 25:6

7   Wagner, *Nine Lenses*, 271.

8   Heb. 13:5

→ **Pray**

Father, help me to see that I am already home. Though my life has had many highs and lows, You've been with me every step of the way. Thank You for removing the angels and flaming sword from the gate of Eden. Through Your Son, Jesus, I now have access to return to the garden and walk with You unashamed.

Day 1 Reflections:

When are the few times you have truly felt like you belonged—either in a place or with a group of people?

_____

_____

_____

_____

What triggers your feelings of alienation?

_____

_____

_____

_____

What makes you think you are unlovable?

_____

_____

_____

_____

→ **Respond**

Search for, listen to, and meditate on "Four," inspired by the Enneagram Type 4, from the Sleeping At Last project.[9]

9   Ryan O'Neal, "Sleeping At Last," Sleeping At Last, 2016, http://sleepingatlast.com.

Day 2:

The Missing Piece

For you formed my inward parts; you knitted me together in my mother's

womb. I praise you, for I am fearfully and wonderfully made. Wonderful are

your works; my soul knows it very well.

—Psalm 139:13-14

"It was missing a piece. And it was not happy."

These are the first words of author Shel Silverstein's charming fable about a circular creature that is missing a piece of itself. So sure it was meant to be complete, it sets out, singing:

> It was missing a piece. And it was not happy. So it set off in search of its missing piece.
>
> –Shel Silverstein[1]

Oh, I'm lookin' for
my missin' piece
I'm lookin' for my missin' piece
Hi-dee-ho, here I go
lookin' for my missin' piece[2]

---

1   Shel Silverstein, *The Missing Piece* (United Kingdom: HarperCollins, 1976).

2   "The Missing Piece," The Prindle Institute for Ethics, accessed May 11, 2021, https://www.prindleinstitute.org/books/the-missing-piece/.

On this dangerous quest to complete itself—falling into holes and bumping into walls, testing and trying many different potential matches—the almost-circle finally finds the perfect wedge. But with the circle complete, it no longer has a mouth to sing and finds itself rolling much too fast to talk to a worm or smell a butterfly. Its belief of completion has left it unable to travel slow enough to receive life as it came. So, it puts down the missing piece and decides to keep searching, ultimately finding completion in the search itself.

The Individualist is also on a never-ending search for their missing piece. Maybe it's an achievement, talent, character quality, or relationship—often it's for something completely unnameable. They often cannot

> In Christ, you have all you need to be worthy of love.

identify the object of the search, but the sense of lack is nonetheless overwhelming. This often causes the Four to withdraw for long periods of time and drive around in the cul-de-sac of introspection, hoping that by looking within, they may find their place and learn why they are so different from everyone else.[3]

Don't get me wrong: introspection is a strength that can lead to personal growth and creativity, but it can also lead to self-destruction. Because it's so easy for you to find what's missing or flawed, there is a temptation to assume that the problem is always you. Having a strong Four wing myself, I am no stranger to the suffocating feelings of inadequacy. After being a pastor for six years, I still feel like something is missing within, keeping me from fulfilling that mysterious calling given so many years ago. Particularly after standing in the spotlight, I feel exposed, continually fearing that one day soon the members of our church will discover who I *really* am and conclude I fall woefully short of what they need in a shepherd. Do you know that kind of fear and feeling?

One of the reasons I wrote this book is to pull up the shades and shine the light on the wonderful qualities you already possess. You are far more loved than you know. I'll say it again: *You are far more loved than you know.* You, who are so adept at uncovering the beauty of the world around, are often the most blind to your own divine design—but others are not.

---

3   Don Riso and Russ Hudson, *Personality Types: Using the Enneagram for Self-Discovery* (HMH Books, 1996), 137.

In the beginning, God created the world and saw that it was "very good."[4] This includes you. You are not some product that must be recalled because of manufacturer defects, for you were woven together in your mother's womb by the Divine Artist. You are *very good*—complete. Even that feeling of lack and that drive to search the ends of the earth is a gift: a call to immerse yourself in the wonder and beauty of your Creator's very good world.

The Good News for Individualists is your search for completion is not your identity. Your worth is not tied to what is unfinished within but in your Source. Whatever goodness you feel you lack has been fully credited to your account: "For our sake he made him to be sin who knew no sin, so that in him we might become the righteousness of God."[5] In Christ, you have all you need to be worthy of love. Continue the search, continue to look deep within, but never lose sight of the One whose completeness fills every part of you.

→ Pray

Father, help me to see that I am already whole. You are my missing piece. Forgive me for calling myself flawed when You've called me "good." Rather than thinking long and hard about my deficiencies, I will think about how fearfully and wonderfully You've made me. As I go about my day, I ask that Your Spirit would free me from self-indulgence and that I would be caught up in what You are doing around me.

---

4   Gen. 1:31

5   2 Cor. 5:21

Day 2 Reflections:

What is the "missing piece" that you feel would complete you?

_____

_____

_____

_____

What would happen if you found that missing piece?

_____

_____

_____

_____

How do you picture the way God is looking at you at this very moment?

_____

_____

_____

_____

→ Respond

Memorize Psalm 139:13-14 to remind yourself that you are incredibly special to God.

Day 3:

The World Needs Artists

In the beginning, God created the heavens and the earth. The earth was without form and void, and darkness was over the face of the deep. And the Spirit of God was hovering over the face of the waters. And God said, "Let there be light," and there was light.

—Genesis 1:1-3

IN THE BEGINNING, ALL IS DARK. THE world is a blank canvas, a sheet of music without any notes. The Divine Artist steps in, hovering above the waters of uncreated chaos, and begins painting, sculpting, and singing creation into existence. With His unfathomable knowledge and limitless power, rocks, animals, and trees, mathematical formulas, scientific laws, and sexuality were written into existence. Out of dirt, God sculpts man and woman and fills them with life in one breath. The Divine Artist steps back and delights in His workmanship.

> The world will be saved by beauty.
> —Fyodor Dostoyevsky[1]

You and I were created to enjoy and imitate God. Though we may not all be artists in the narrow

---

1   Rohr and Ebert, *The Enneagram*, 98.

sense, God gave all mankind the task of stewarding creation—assisting in the cultivating and beatification of all we see.[2] Tailors, janitors, electricians, teachers, and composers all take the raw materials of fabric, brooms, electricity, the alphabet, and sound waves and emulate the Creator by turning it all into a work of art.[3]

No matter your vocation, as an Individualist you have been uniquely created to reflect the *imago Dei*[4] by embodying the *originality* of God. Through creative action, you put on display God's mysterious beauty, and through your own authentic vulnerability, you invite others to dwell in the paradoxes of life: triumph and tragedy, rejoicing and mourning, sanctification and suffering.

The power unleashed in your creative expressions does nothing less than touch and transform the human heart. Even if you think you are exercising creativity for personal enjoyment or therapeutic reasons, your endeavors often have far-reaching, universal implications. Artists have a knack for giving us glimpses of our Lost Paradise; they set the indefinable aspects of heaven and earth before our eyes in ways that are inescapable.

> The purpose of our brilliant creativity should ultimately point people to the Divine Artist behind the world's canvas.

Timothy Keller, in his brilliant essay "Why We Need Artists," makes the case that creatives offer us a cognitive leg-up into contemplative truth. When artists are deployed, we are moved beyond the realm of rationality into the realm of praise.[5] Martin Luther himself wrote nearly 100 songs so that people could sing the truths they were learning in the pews. Pastor John Starke explains, "Luther combined both high art and folk music in his hymns so as to make the theology of the Reformation part of the everyday culture of the people. The result was that songs about justification by faith alone and the authority of God's Word were sung in

---

2   Gen. 1:28

3   Timothy Keller, *Every Good Endeavor: Connecting Your Work to God's Work* (United States: Penguin Publishing Group, 2014), 47.

4   Gen. 1:27

5   *It Was Good: Making Art to the Glory of God* (United States: Square Halo Books, 2007), 117-124.

homes by housewives over dirty dishes and in pubs by farmers and mill workers over pints of ale."[6]

Individualists cultivate beauty wherever they are due to a high sensitivity to and standard for aesthetics. Their ideals are often more *aesthetic* than they are ethical—in fact, their ethics are largely informed and confirmed by contemplative (unspeakable) truth.[7] They value beauty and design, so don't expect them to budge in the workplace when others want to sacrifice quality to cut costs. This commitment to originality and design extends even to seemingly minor things like wardrobe. Many Fours tend to set themselves apart by wearing clothes from secondhand shops or boutiques—anything that is not mass-produced.

Fours' unique contributions are a blessing to the world, opening new vistas on the beauty always around. But as C.S. Lewis warns, "The books or the music in which we thought the beauty was located will betray us if we trust to them; it was not in them, it only came through them. ... For they are not the thing itself; they are only the scent of a flower we have not found, the echo of a tune we have not heard, news from a country we have never yet visited."[8] In other words, the purpose of our brilliant creativity should ultimately point people to the Divine Artist behind the world's canvas.

The Good News for Individualists is that your gifts are of valuable worth. After the Hebrews were liberated from slavery in Egypt, they decided to build the tabernacle as their place of worship in the desert. The Lord told Moses to choose a craftsman named Bezalel to build it with breathtaking, artistic design. This talented craftsman (not a religious leader mind you) was filled with the Spirit and commissioned by God![9] Know that the same Spirit who hovered over the waters in creation and filled Bezalel with creative talent to point people to God has commissioned you today to create meaningful work that produces awe and wonder at the glories of our Creator.

---

6   John Starke, "The Forgotten Influence of Martin Luther," The Gospel Coalition, February 8, 2012, https://www.thegospelcoalition.org/article/the-forgotten-influence-of-martin-luther/.

7   Claudio Naranjo, *Character and Neurosis: An Integrative View* (United States: Gateways/IDHHB, 1994), 123.

8   *It was Good*, 119-120.

9   Ex. 31:1-11

→ **Pray**

Father, forgive me for looking in the mirror of my own aesthetic needs too much. I've served my image, not Yours. Help me to see the beauty already present within me as *Your* gift; cleanse my heart of every inclination to steal the glory You deserve and to better reflect the beauty I see back to You. Fill me with the Holy Spirit to produce excellent works that draw others' attention to Your beauty.

Day 3 Reflections:

Which words most reflect the image of God in you? Deep, tasteful, empathetic, imaginative, creative, unique, different, intuitive, and expressive? What other qualities come to mind?[10]

_____

_____

_____

How do you use aesthetics to enhance your home, workplace, or wardrobe in order to create the right mood or atmosphere?

_____

_____

_____

How can you bring more depth, beauty, and mystery to the world? How do you already do this?

_____

_____

_____

→ **Respond**

Search for an image or famous piece of art that best describes your life now. Then find one that best describes what you want to represent your life. Share it with someone.

10   Scott Loughrige, Clare M. Loughrige, Douglas A. Calhoun, and Adele Ahlberg Calhoun, *Spiritual Rhythms For The Enneagram: A Handbook for Harmony and Transformation* (Downers Grove, IL: InterVarsity Press, 2019), 112.

Day 4:

The Friend Inside

"And you shall love the LORD your God with all your heart and with all your

soul and with all your mind and with all your strength.' The second is this: 'You

shall love your neighbor as yourself.' There is no other commandment greater

than these."

—Mark 12:30-31

DO YOU LIKE YOURSELF? TO PUT IT another way: Would you choose someone just like you to be your friend? The average Individualist is prone to having a poor self-image due to the nagging sense of feeling inadequate, of deep, inconsolable lack. Since the best things about themselves are often "hidden in plain sight" and often don't match their own standards of aesthetic perfection, they may have an unshakable conviction that they are a failure or "damaged goods."[2]

> For me to be a saint means to be myself.
>
> –Thomas Merton[1]

Individualists are deeply idealistic. They paint the perfect picture in their own heads of who

---

1 Thomas Merton and Sue Monk Kidd, *New Seeds of Contemplation* (United Kingdom: New Directions Book, 2007), 31.

2 Maitri, *The Spiritual Dimension,* 144.

they (and everyone else) ought to be. The problem is that this image is unattainable. Although there is a sort of joy in the longing to fulfill their standards of perfection, the inevitable failure to make the grade can have destructive consequences for many, creating a self-fulfilling prophecy of lost relationships.[3,4] The fact is, they have problems with love because they don't love themselves.

Throughout his time in office, President Abraham Lincoln endured much criticism during the brutal years of the Civil War. Though he was not a perfect leader, one of his many admirable strengths was his integrity. He refused to compromise on his values to gain more political favor. Lincoln famously said, "I desire so to conduct the affairs of this administration that if at the end ... I have lost every other friend on earth, I shall at least have one friend left, and that friend shall be down inside of me."[5] For Lincoln, what mattered most was self-friendship. If he didn't love himself first, then no amount of friendships would fill the void.[6]

> God's love does not fluctuate by how close or far away you are from your perceived ideal self.

When a religious leader asked Jesus what the greatest commandment was, He replies, "Love the Lord your God with all your heart," but He continues, saying "The second is this: 'You shall love your neighbor as yourself.'"[7] What strikes me are the words "as yourself." Jesus makes the assumption that we love ourselves or that we have some inkling of our place as beloved children of God and, therefore, of our overwhelming value to the Divine Source. What many fail to see is how our lack of self-love and acceptance is a denial of God and effectively an act of pride.

You can't truly love someone with the self-forgetful, humble love of Christ until you accept how much God loves you first. One of the apostle Paul's most

---

3   Ibid, 143.

4   Riso and Hudson, *Personality Types*, 171-172.

5   Kate Louise Roberts, *Hoyt's New Cyclopedia of Practical Quotations* (United Kingdom: Funk & Wagnalls Company), 1922.

6   This Abraham Lincoln quote and self-friendship discussion appeared on Ian Morgan Cron's interview with Brian McLaren, *Author Brian McLaren on Internal Friendship (Enneagram 4) [S03-037]*, podcast audio, April 9, 2020, https://www.typologypodcast.com/podcast/2020/09/04/episode03-037/brianmclaren.

7   Mark 12:30-31

incredible prayers was that we "may have strength to comprehend with all the saints what is the breadth and length and height and depth, and to know the love of Christ that surpasses knowledge … ."[8]

The Good News for Individualists is that the Christian story is about how the Father so deeply cared for His creation that He physically entered the narrative as His Son, demonstrating His love through sacrificial love.[9] The beauty of the gospel is that He can declare sinners to be saints. As Chrystal Evans Hurst says, "You are allowed to be both a masterpiece and a work in progress simultaneously."[10] God's love does not fluctuate by how close or far away you are from your perceived ideal self. It is secure in Christ. For in Christ, you are a new creation.[11] What is needed to combat negative self-esteem isn't a higher view of yourself but an accurate view of yourself hidden in the love of Christ.

When you are able to enjoy who you are because of *whose* you are, you can begin to take genuine pleasure in how God wired you to bring His beauty to the world. Remember, friendship with yourself will set the tone for all of your relationships. Therefore, open your hands to catch God's overflowing pleasure today. As the saying goes, "You can't pour from an empty cup."

→ Pray

Father, You are love. Forgive me for being overly self-critical and downplaying Your grace toward me. Help me to fix my eyes continually on Your beautiful gaze so that I might reflect Your love back to You and onto others. Strengthen my spiritual muscles today to comprehend more and more just how scandalous Your perfect love is toward imperfect people.

---

8   Eph. 3:18-19

9   Rom. 3:23

10   Chrystal Evans Hurst, *She's Still There: Rescuing the Girl in You* (United States: Zondervan, 2017).

11   2 Cor. 5:17

Day 4 Reflections:

Do you love yourself? What positive attributes would you use to describe yourself?

_____

_____

_____

_____

What lies are you believing about yourself? What concrete evidence do you have for believing them?

_____

_____

_____

_____

What does it mean for God to love you? How would you define the real impact of that idea on your life?

_____

_____

_____

_____

➜ Respond

This may be a little uncomfortable, but ask a friend to share what they like about you.

Day 5:

Empathy and More
Superpowers

I am reminded of your sincere faith, a faith that dwelt first in your grandmother

Lois and your mother Eunice and now, I am sure, dwells in you as well. For this

reason I remind you to fan into flame the gift of God, which is in you through

the laying on of my hands, for God gave us a spirit not of fear but of power and

love and self-control.

—2 Timothy 1:5-7

IF YOU HAVE EVER BEEN CAMPING, YOU'RE probably accustomed to starting fires (or watching your "outdoorsy" friend do it). Dried leaves or twigs are laid down to kindle the fire, followed by increasingly larger sticks and logs. Once ablaze, you can finally get to the good part—sitting under the stars and soaking up a good conversation. Yet all too soon, the once-roaring flames begin to die. Rather than start the process all over again, all you need to

> Situation hopeless,
> but not serious.
> —Robert Shaw[1]

---

1   Alice Fryling, *Mirror for the Soul: A Christian Guide to the Enneagram* (United States: InterVarsity Press, 2017), 67.

do is bend down and blow on the glowing embers to fan them back into a flame. Within seconds, the fire will be roaring again.[2]

In his second letter to young Timothy, the apostle Paul challenged his son in the faith to not let his fire die. Timothy was exhorted to "fan" into flame "the gift of God," which his mentor laid upon him. This gift's most vital ember is a deep knowing of the love God is eternally pouring out on all people. A person living out of this wholeness can set an entire community ablaze—and a community can ignite the world. Paul did not bestow divine love on the young man but opened his eyes to what was there all along. Timothy's flame, unique according to his own giftedness and vocation, offered light and warmth to his people.

You might be asking, "What would it look like for *me* to fan this same gift in my heart?" As a Four, one of your unique gifts to society is empathy. The suffering you've endured helps you connect to the suffering of others and provide a safe, comforting, non-judgmental space. You are not afraid of grief or our powerlessness to end it, and so, you make an ideal fellow mourner. Showing up to "mourn with those who mourn,"[3] is an intuitive act for you. Whereas many people back away

> Christ's love inflames your capacity to be thoughtful, understanding, apologetic, gentle, cordial, self-sacrificing, humble, empathetic, and attentive.

from hard emotions or seek to find "solutions" to end the pain, you lean in and provide nurturing support. A true believer in suffering and love's combined power to create lasting transformation, you derive pleasure from walking with others through the shadow of death. As one Four shared, "There is nothing as beautiful as the landscape of intimacy, growth and development."[4]

This emotional sensitivity is a superpower that allows you to connect in deep ways with friends, co-workers, and loved ones. Your "grief X-ray vision" offers

---

2   "What Does It Mean to Fan into Flame the Gift of God?," Bibles for America Blog, July 20, 2018, https://blog.biblesforamerica.org/fan-into-flame-the-gift-of-god/.

3   Rom. 12:15 NIV

4   Beatrice Chestnut, *The 9 Types of Leadership: Mastering the Art of People in the 21st Century Workplace* (Post Hill Press, 2017), 138.

insight into those around, allowing you to notice who is connected and who is alone or hurting. This allows you to "bring people together, sensitively mediate conflicts, and name emotional issues that need to be faced so teams can become more cohesive."[5]

Another superpower is your aesthetic sensibility. Your eye gravitates toward the beautiful unseen—the lovely, commendable, and excellent qualities in the world—and seeks to highlight them in poetic ways.[6] Loving the creative process, you offer your artistic eye to projects when needed, provide an abundance of innovative ideas, and help others unleash their creativity. When you are doing something you find meaningful and significant, you increase the temperature of the room with your passion,[7] adding "so much color and depth and texture to our lives."[8]

The Good News for Individualists is that Christ's love inflames your capacity to be thoughtful, understanding, apologetic, gentle, cordial, self-sacrificing, humble, empathetic, and attentive.[9] Your natural gifts are part of a grand plan to restore humanity, mirroring Christ's mission to bring depth to a world that all too often rejects introspection and suppresses hard, paradoxical truths. Just as Jesus had compassion on the hurting, you also show up and offer your healing presence. Just as Jesus fully embraced His humanity, you too can help the world understand "the depths to which human beings can descend, as well as the heights to which they can be swept up."[10]

Remember, you didn't start the fire, so you can't put it out! Just as the disciples on the road to Emmaus exclaimed that their hearts were burning after being with Jesus, so too have our hearts been ignited by the Holy Spirit and kept ablaze by walking with Jesus. Our only job is to keep fanning the flame!

---

5   Ibid, 145.

6   Phil. 4:8

7   Chestnut, *The 9 Types of Leadership*, 151-152.

8   Suzanne Stabile, *The Path Between Us: An Enneagram Journey to Healthy Relationships* (IVP Books, 2018), 120.

9   Naranjo, *Character and Neurosis*, 121.

10   Riso and Hudson, *Personality Types*, 138.

→ Pray

Father, I wouldn't be here without You or the friends and family who have invested in me. Thank You for giving me faithful people who have prayed for, taught, disciplined, modeled for, and led me. Help me to walk slowly through this world and be a healing presence, pouring out the fire of Your love on a world cold with pain.

Day 5 Reflections:

Paul asked Timothy to take inventory of the spiritual deposit made by his mother and grandmother. What spiritual truths and gifts have been passed down to you from your family and/or mentors?

Which of the strengths above have been affirmed the most throughout your life?

What's one thing you can do to ignite and develop your gifts?

→ Respond

Identify your strengths and give examples of how you are already using them.

Day 6:

Kaleidoscope of Emotions

Jesus wept.

—John 11:35

"JESUS WEPT." THOSE WORDS REPEATED THROUGH MY lowered head as I sat at my desk, my own tears welling up. A long road of infertility had rocked my marriage, leaving crushed dreams and hopes deferred. Experiences like this are difficult for anyone, but when the ones from whom you seek comfort grieve differently, it can add alienation and loneliness to the pain.

For years, my wife cried and cried, unable to believe we'd ever see a miracle, and to this day, still no miracle. I didn't cry, but instead kept telling her to "have faith." Looking back, I can see now that what I had was not *faith* but *naivety*. I suppressed my emotions by naively assuming everything would work out. But this was just an unconscious strategy to sweep things under the rug. In so doing, I suppressed Lindsey's

> Though our feelings come and go, His love for us does not.
>
> –C.S. Lewis[1]

---

1   C. S. Lewis, *The Complete C.S. Lewis Signature Classics* (United Kingdom: HarperCollins, 2007), 111.

pain, dodged her emotions, failed to offer God's presence, and held fast to stoicism when I should have been sowing tears.

Thankfully, we joined a redemption group of believers who felt stuck in various ways. During one of our sessions, the leader pointed his finger at me and sternly said, "David was a man who grieved and was called a man after God's own heart. You haven't done that." Those words broke me, and the next morning I read the story of Lazarus. When I came across the powerfully short line, "Jesus wept," I heard God

> You can bring every emotion to Jesus without fear of getting rejected. Your emotions aren't too much for Him.

tell me: "Lindsey's tears are My tears." And for the first time since we began our struggle, I put my head down and wept, crying out:

I have not cried, but now I'm crying.
I have not seen You clearly, but now I see.
Glorify Yourself in me as Your Spirit replaces my stoicism with sorrow.
Make much of Yourself in my life as I behold Your Son,
A Man of Sorrows, acquainted with grief.

I have come to understand that strong emotions, even painful ones, are a gift from God, bringing depth to our lives. They allow us to feel loss when a loved one passes away, conviction when we rebel, disappointment when others fail us, or pleasure when with good friends.

Using the human body as a metaphor, I think of Individualists as playing the role of the central nervous system. Just as our nerves transport important messages back and forth between our body and brain, Fours teach us about the pains and pleasures of life. You, as a Four, have a way of raising our communal dopamine and serotonin levels, compelling us to stop and smell the roses.

While your impressive, emotional intelligence can be a blessing, it can easily feel like a curse. As one Four shared, "It ain't easy going through life feeling all of the feelings."[2] I once heard someone equate a Four's head with a powerball machine with dozens of emotions flying around in circles all at once!

Because you are feeling things deeply all the time, you can easily have an identity crisis. As Enneagram expert Ian Cron notes, "Fours don't have feelings; they are their feelings."[3] When your identity is based upon a shifting thing like feelings, you will soon find your peace and self-worth swept away. But Jesus promises that those who build their house on the rock of truth—of the eternal, unyielding love of God—will live securely.[4] With Jesus' help, you can live out of a foundation of love and steward your emotions without *becoming* them.

The Good News for Individualists is that Jesus was a kaleidoscope of emotions, able to express the entire spectrum of human warmth and love, anger and frustration, grief and loss. When we say that Jesus was "fully human," we mean that He plumbed the depths of the human experience. He experienced it all like us—only more so. Jesus felt deep compassion toward the sick and infirm, anger toward evil and hypocrisy, grief over death and loneliness, and distress over humanity's waywardness. You can bring every emotion to Jesus without fear of rejection. Your emotions aren't too much for Him.

→ Pray

Father, thank You for giving me a love that I can *feel*—one that surpasses knowledge. Forgive me for hiding in my feelings and using them as a place of refuge. Thank You for sending Jesus to redeem me from over-identifying with my emotions and giving me something solid to stand on. By Your Spirit, allow me to use my feelings as a guide rather than being controlled by them.

---

2   Ian Morgan Cron, *The Road Back to You Study Guide* (United States: InterVarsity Press, 2016), 38.

3   Cron and Stabile, *The Road Back to You*, 155.

4   Matt. 7:24-27

Day 6 Reflections:

When have you used your feelings to positively influence others?

_____

_____

_____

_____

How does overindulging negative or positive emotions meet your desire to feel special or self-sacrificial?

_____

_____

_____

How can you prevent your feelings from calling the shots in your life?

_____

_____

_____

_____

➜ Respond

Write down an emotion you most identify with right now and give it a name: Elation, Fury, Envy, Suffering, and so on. Now, imagine yourself setting it ten feet away. Give it a size, shape, and color. Notice what changes when you get distance from it. Now, respond to this emotion by either telling it goodbye, taking it to God, or creating a plan of action.[5]

---

5 The idea of giving your emotion a shape comes from Lindsey Antin, "More Than a Feeling: How Over-Identification Gets in the Way," Good Therapy, February 23, 2016, https://www.goodtherapy.org/blog/more-than-a-feeling-how-over-identification-gets-in-the-way-0223164.

Day 7:

Spears of Envy

... love does not envy ...

—1 Corinthians 13:4b

DEMARICK WAS A CAMPUS MINISTER AND MY first spiritual mentor. He was an incredibly gifted communicator who helped me start a Greek life ministry on our college campus, and I often found myself unconsciously envious of his gifts. Though my own role was significant—casting vision to other leaders, recruiting dozens of students, and organizing our weekly meeting—I still vividly remember feeling a stinging sense of envy toward Demarick as he spoke one evening. Everyone in the room was captivated and I thought to myself, "Why am I even here? They want *him*, not me." This man I so admired began to morph into an object of envy.

> Envy is the only sin I can think of that is really no fun at all.
>
> –Tilly Dillehay[1]

Envy is what is known as the Individualists's *vice*, or *core weakness*. For the Four, envy is a result of that nagging feeling that you're missing

---

1   Tilly Dillehay, "4 Ways To Conquer Your Envy," The Gospel Coalition, September 26, 2018, https://www.thegospelcoalition.org/article/4-ways-conquer-envy/.

something vital that others seem to naturally possess. You can catch a Four looking upon others and feeling melancholy because, as Ian Cron notes, "They instantly spot who has a more interesting life, a happier family or childhood story, a better job, superior taste, a more privileged education, more distinguishing clothes or unrivaled artistic talent."[2]

Envy makes the grass look greener in others' lives. In the age of social media—when everyone is able to craft the perfect persona—we are even more prone to envy, especially if we take others' staged posts as their whole story.

King Saul was no stranger to feelings of envy. One day, he heard a group of women singing, "Saul has struck down his thousands, and David his ten thousands."[3] The enraged Saul looks upon the young hero playing the lyre and burns with envy (and its natural partner for those in positions of authority: fear). Songwriter Aaron Keys points out the irony: "So you have David, with harp in hand; and you have Saul, with spear in hand. One was an instrument of healing, the other an instrument for hurt. One was used to deliver, the other to destroy. One was a tool for soothing, the other for striking."[4]

> Christ has not given more of Himself to others than He has to you.

David, a loyal servant to God and Saul, holds a lyre in his hands, providing a form of musical therapy for the king's troubled soul. But Saul, filled with envy and fear of David's success—proof of God's presence with the young man—hurls a spear at David possibly to pin down the source of his insecurity. David evades him—twice.[5]

What's in your hand? Has the passion of envy ever run so freely in your own life that you not only wanted something (extrinsic or intrinsic) someone had, but also wanted them to pay for having it? When left unchecked, the spears of envy

---

2   Cron and Stabile, *The Road Back to You*, 153.

3   1 Sam. 18:7b

4   Aaron Keys, "Harps or Spears," September 14, 2011, https://www.aaronkeyes.com/blog/2011/9/14/harps-or-spears.

5   1 Sam. 18:10-12

are inevitably directed toward the very best people in our lives—as I did with Demarick, and Saul did with David.[6]

The Good News for Individualists is that Christ has not given more of Himself to others than He has to you. Scarcity and zero-sum thinking is the same lie the accuser used to lead our ancestors to *take* the fruit out of suspicious envy, losing sight of the divine abundance all around. God is not holding out on you as the serpent would lead you to believe; His abundant love and acceptance is poured out on all without favoritism.

You can stop playing the "but" game by saying things like, "I'm empathetic, but he is a better communicator" or "I have a great career, but she has the perfect marriage." See yourself through God's lens of significance today and be the miracle you were made to be. Trust Him that you don't need more from the world, but that the world needs more of you.

→ Pray

Father, You have graciously given me all things in Christ. I choose today to put off envy and put on love. Grow my appreciation for what I have—physically and internally. Let me admire those who have what I don't. Help me to stop exaggerating others' lives and find contentment now that my life is hidden in You.

---

6   Maitri, *The Spiritual Dimension*, 142.

Day 7 Reflections:

Who do you envy and why?

_____

_____

_____

_____

What unique qualities, close relationships, or possessions do you have that others might envy?

_____

_____

_____

If God graciously distributes unique gifts to each of us according to His wisdom, how should that change the way we view ourselves and treat others?

_____

_____

_____

→ Respond

Pick someone you envy and pray for their success, thank God for their gifts, publicly affirm them, and seek to enjoy their gifts without making any comparisons.

Day 8:

Man of Sorrows

He was despised and rejected by men, a man of sorrows and acquainted with grief; and as one from whom men hide their faces he was despised, and we esteemed him not.

—Isaiah 53:3

"LIFE WOULDN'T BE SO HARD IF WE didn't expect it to be so easy."

> God whispers to us in our pleasures, speaks in our consciences, but shouts in our pains. It is His megaphone to rouse a deaf world.
>
> —C.S. Lewis[1]

My summer mission leader, Dan, first shared that important axiom with me as a college student. In my almost four decades of life, I've experienced the grief of losing loved ones, the pain of infertility, the distress that comes with having a child on the autism spectrum, and the sorrow of officiating funerals for members of my church. I'm keenly aware that we are living in the "already but not yet" kingdom. Can you relate?

---

1 Clyde S. Kilby, *The Christian World of C. S. Lewis* (United States: William B. Eerdmans Publishing Company, 1995), 68.

One of our culture's most popular alternatives to the path of Jesus is the prosperity gospel, known as the "health and wealth gospel." This dangerous rejection of life's fullness proclaims that the kingdom has been inaugurated and fully consummated. In other words, you can claim for yourself a life of material plenty, without sickness, poverty, or suffering right now—if you just have enough faith. But the Bible leads us in a different direction, toward a host of suffering protagonists: Joseph, Moses, Hannah, David,

> As someone who walks in the footsteps of the Man of Sorrows, do not be ashamed of your tears.

Ruth, Job, Mary, and Paul to name a few. From these inspiring men and women, we learn about the normalcy—and *necessity*—of suffering.

I'm assuming that to embrace a theology of suffering is not hard for you. Suzanne Stabile explains, "Fours have the gifts and the grace to hold both beauty and pain without the need to choose one over the other."[2] They are very comfortable dealing with the emotional intensity found in life-or-death situations, emergencies, suicide hotlines, and other crises. Ian Cron puts it this way: "Most Fours could teach Anguish as a Second Language. They're drawn to all things tragic, and their talk style is lament."[3]

How Fours handle their own suffering can look vastly different. Some are long-suffering, tending to deny or suppress their pain, living unaware of the source of the shadow constantly tugging on their heart. Others express their suffering outwardly and "wear it on their sleeve." If left unexamined, this pain creates a person in a state of perpetual, public grief, drawing on others' energy. However, when properly channeled, these people's grief can be sublimated into an outflow of transformed energy, such as art capable of conveying the depth and subtlety of the human experience. Still others project their suffering onto people more aggressively to counter painful feelings of inferiority;[4] in states of unhealth, they believe "the way to happiness is through tears"[5] and can become like children who

---

2   Stabile, *The Path Between Us*, 126.

3   Cron and Stabile, *The Road Back to You*, 154.

4   Beatrice Chestnut, *The Complete Enneagram: 27 Paths to Greater Self-Knowledge* (Berkeley, CA: She Writes Press, 2013), 285.

5   Ibid, 289.

use their tears to get a parent to rescue them, repeatedly sharing past stories of suffering to draw others to them.

The Good News for Individualists is that our God is a Man of Sorrows who came to rescue us through life's pain. This Suffering Servant carried the weight of all our sorrow and shame, wholly healing us by His wounds.[6] As the old hymn goes:

> Oh, that old rugged cross, so despised by the world,
>> Has a wondrous attraction for me;
> For the dear Lamb of God left His glory above,
>> To bear it to dark Calvary.[7]

The cross, a symbol of death, is at the very center of our faith. Jesus pursued "the joy that was set before him"[8] by first walking the path of pain, not prosperity. In so doing, He set the example for us to follow: to enter into the world's pain, receiving its darkness and transforming it into healing light. The apostle Peter left us this exhortation: " ... Christ also suffered for you, leaving you an example, so that you might follow in his steps,"[9] later following his own words and being crucified. According to tradition, Peter was crucified upside down because he didn't feel worthy to die in the same way as his Lord. Like our Lord and the long tradition of those who walked the way of suffering, we must avoid anyone in this world that promises us only comfort, leisure, and excessive stability. A disciple of Christ is fundamentally one who suffers.

As someone who walks in the footsteps of the Man of Sorrows, do not be ashamed of your tears. As the thirteenth century Sufi poet Rumi explains, "Sorrow prepares you for joy. It violently sweeps everything out of your house so that new joy can find space to enter."[10] With this mindset, go and show the world today what it looks like to be *fully* human—holding both beauty and pain together.

---

6   Isa. 53:4-6

7   George Bennard, "The Old Rugged Cross," Hymnal.net, https://www.hymnal.net/en/hymn/h/618.

8   Heb. 12:2b

9   1 Pet. 2:21b

10   Chestnut, *The Complete Enneagram*, 267.

→ **Pray**

Father, my soul is comforted as I see Your Son, Jesus, weeping at Lazarus' funeral. As I find my way through a stoic society, remind me that tears are Your gift to me so that I can feel what You feel. Do not let me waste my tears, but sow my tears into this dry land filled with other hurting people who need to be nourished with empathy.

Day 8 Reflections:

When have you felt "less than" for showing your tears? How does it feel to know Jesus weeps with you?

_____

_____

_____

_____

Do you tend to wear your suffering on your sleeve, suffer silently, or project it onto others with a megaphone?

_____

_____

_____

_____

How does a prosperity gospel without suffering distort our view of God and make us less human?

_____

_____

_____

_____

→ **Respond**

Pursue someone who feels rejected or is experiencing low-self esteem and offer to sit with them.

Day 9:

Woe Is Me

And I said: "Woe is me! For I am lost; for I am a man of unclean lips, and I

dwell in the midst of a people of unclean lips; for my eyes have seen the King,

*the L*ORD *of hosts!"*

—Isaiah 6:5

SOME SAY JUDAS BETRAYED JESUS FOR MONEY. Others speculate that being a Zealot, he wanted to force his non-violent Messiah to finally stand up to their Roman oppressors and seize His role as God-ordained, earthly king. Regardless of Judas' motivation, when his heavy pockets led to the Messiah's condemnation, death became the only way he could see out of his unbearable shame. Disgusted with himself, he was *hopeless* that God could ever delight in him again and sought a final end to his suffering.

> Forgive yourself for not knowing what you didn't know before you learned it.
>
> —Maya Angelou

Peter was another disciple who sat at Jesus' feet, witnessed His miracles, and betrayed Him on that final dark night. Earlier in the evening, Peter emphatically proclaimed he would die with Jesus before denying Him, but it only took the words of a young girl for Peter to invoke a curse on himself and swear three times that he didn't know Jesus. At the rooster's crows, Peter remembers his Master's words and weeps bitterly.[1]

The end of the story for these two ashamed men looks vastly different. Judas takes his own life, alone at the end; while Peter is reconciled to his Lord and community, becoming the de facto leader of the first century church. What happened, you ask? Sitting in his shame, Peter is reminded who Jesus is and becomes *hopeful* that he can come to see himself as his ever-loving God does.

Shame is the dominant emotion for the Individualist, often functioning as a sort of drone note, holding the same, low, steady tone throughout their lives. Therefore, it must be confronted in order to grow into greater freedom and maturity. Shame is a powerful tool in the hands of the accuser, whether overtly proclaimed by the surrounding world or from within, as it so often happens for the Four. As Sandra Maitri pointed out, "The degree of maliciousness and venom that Fours can display toward others is minimal compared to what they heap on themselves."[2]

> God bridges the gap of perceived inadequacy so that His people may be ready for service.

More than any other personality type, Fours say they feel that others can sense their nakedness and vulnerability. In many ways, this assumed exposure is a sort of shadow to one of this type's greatest gifts: *authenticity.* This struggle with an awareness of exposure reminds me of the prophet Isaiah's vision of the Lord in the temple. Standing in the great and majestic presence of the Holy One, he sees both the full, infinite perfection of God, recognizes his own all-too finite shortcomings, and cries out, "Woe is me!"

In Isaiah's greatest moment of vulnerability and accompanying shame, God acts as God *always* does: bridging the gap of perceived inadequacy so that His people may be ready for service: "Then one of the seraphim flew to me, having in his hand a burning coal that he had taken with tongs from the altar. And he touched my mouth and said: 'Behold, this has touched your lips; your guilt is taken away,

---

1 Matt. 26:69-75

2 Maitri, *The Spiritual Dimension,* 143.

and your sin atoned for.'"[3] Rather than getting burned with judgement, the coals lead to a cleansing. They purged the prophet of his shame, restoring confidence within him to stand up and shout, "Here I am! Send me."[4]

The Good News for Individualists is that in Christ, our greatest acts of rebellion become an invitation for an even greater experience of loving-kindness. Much as Peter's denial *and* reconciliation occured around the inviting warmth of a charcoal fire,[5] the Father has taken the burning coals from the sacrifice of His Son and has cleansed us fully and finally of all our past, present, and future shames. He wants to reach into the darkest crevices in your soul today, where you feel the most fearful of exposure, and heal you through and through. He invites you to stop assuaging your shame through negative self-talk, self-harm, or by taking refuge in the sort of melancholy feelings leading only to more shame. Like Peter, if you have the courage to come back to Jesus after your all-too human failings are made known, you will receive tender mercy and hope for a fresh start.

→ Pray

Father, I want to see myself the way You see me. There is a lot that I am ashamed about, but I praise You today for drawing near to me when I feel unworthy and removing all stains of shame. You sent Jesus to defeat shame and free me from it's dreadful effects. By the power of the Holy Spirit, help me keep my eyes off of my sin and place them on my Savior.

---

3   Isa. 6:6-7

4   Isa. 6:8

5   John 18:18; 21:9

Day 9 Reflections:

When do you feel ashamed? Who makes you feel ashamed the most?

_____

_____

_____

_____

How have you used your gift of vulnerability to "get ahead of" your own shame?

_____

_____

_____

_____

What would you have the courage to do for the Lord if you had no fear of being shamed?

_____

_____

_____

_____

➜ Respond

When you start feeling like something is wrong with you, ask, "How do I know this is true?" Write out the lie you are believing alongside biblical truths to combat this false narrative.

Day 10:

The Misunderstood Misfit

O LORD, you have searched me and known me! You know when I sit down and

when I rise up; you discern my thoughts from afar. You search out my path and

my lying down and are acquainted with all my ways.

—Psalm 139:1-3

IN THE CLASSIC TELEVISION SPECIAL *RUDOLF THE* Red-Nosed Reindeer, we encounter the Island of Misfit Toys. This group of toys all have a strange quirk about them, such as the "Charlie in the Box," a train with square wheels, and a sinking boat. When Rudolf accidentally stumbles upon this island with his friends Hermey and Yukon Cornelius, he learns that these quarantined "misfits" have been waiting years for suitable owners.

> The Island of Misfit Toys allows us to imagine that maybe our flaws are actually just our uniqueness misunderstood.
>
> −Unknown

As a Four, you likely know the feeling of being a misfit—living separate from your family, friends, and wider world, perpetually waiting for someone to come along who truly understands you. Individualists say they commonly feel misunderstood, dismissed by others as being too difficult, and undervalued for what they bring to the table.[1]

Whereas some people say about themselves, "what you see is what you get," Cron and Stabile note that when it comes to Fours, "what you see is never what you get."[2] They are multilayered, deeply intriguing, always wrestling with paradoxes, and living comfortably in the mysteries that most people avoid. When it comes to the workplace, Fours may feel like misfits when they bring their full range of emotions and intuitions in a corporate—or even non-profit—environment that's "all about the numbers."

Once there was a young girl who wanted to give a unique Christmas gift to her father. After a long search, she finally came across an exotic parakeet that was so special it could speak five different languages and whistle the entire *Peanuts* theme song. The young girl emptied her checking and savings account to buy it because she wanted her father to know just how much he meant to her. She shipped the exotic parakeet to her father on Christmas day and called him to ask, "Did you get my gift?" Her dad replied, "Oh, yes, it was delicious!"[3]

> God understands us better than we understand ourselves.

Her father obviously didn't know what to do with this special gift. Do you sometimes feel like the parakeet that others don't know what to do with? Jesus knows how you feel. He and his cousin, John the Baptist, were prophets who knew what it was to be "never accepted in [their] hometown."[4] Both were young, single men who chose a life of itinerant homelessness.

Jesus purposefully chose friends from particularly suspect or outcast communities: tax collectors and prostitutes, zealots and women. The religious leaders were scandalized, misunderstanding both men as blasphemers and law-breakers, and

---

1   Chestnut, *The 9 Types of Leadership*, 156.

2   Cron and Stabile, *The Road Back to You*, 155.

3   This story was adapted from a sermon illustration by Pastor Tony Evans, *Tony Evans' Book of Illustrations: Stories, Quotes, and Anecdotes from More Than 30 Years of Preaching and Public Speaking* (United States: Moody Publishers, 2009), 117-118.

4   Luke 4:24 NIV

even demon-possessed.[5] The leaders were so unable to understand such misfits that they accused both of committing mutually exclusive crimes: "For John came neither eating nor drinking, and they say, 'He has a demon'; the Son of Man came eating and drinking, and they say, 'Look, a glutton and a drunkard, a friend of tax collectors and sinners!' Yet wisdom is vindicated by her deeds."[6] Though Jesus is the Son of God who came to rescue us, the great tragedy is the Pharisees misunderstood Him to be a false prophet and instigator of insurrection and crucified Him on a criminal's cross.

The Good News for Individualists is that God understands us better than we understand ourselves. Our Creator is far more complex than we are; we are not a mystery to Him. As the Psalmist rejoices, "O LORD, you have searched me and known me! ... and are acquainted with all my ways."[7] Jesus is our great High Priest, who has lived and died as one of us and is able to sympathize with us when no one else can.[8] Even more, when our feelings are heavy and we can't put them into words, Christ's gift of presence steps in: " ... the Spirit helps us in our weakness. For we do not know what to pray for as we ought, but the Spirit himself intercedes for us with groanings too deep for words."[9]

Very few people will ever fully understand you and how you see the world. That's a reality you'll have to live with, but it does not have to be bad news. Your unique view of the world is a gift that can open new vistas of beauty. Believe it or not, your loved ones see more clearly than you think and almost always have a higher view of yourself than you do. Receive them as God's gift that they will always love you for who you are, not for how deep or significant you become.

---

5   Matt. 12:24

6   Matt. 11:18-19 NRSV

7   Ps. 139:1,3

8   Heb. 4:14

9   Rom. 8:26

Day 10 Reflections:

When in your past have you felt like a misfit?

_____

_____

_____

What triggers your feelings of alienation?

_____

_____

_____

How does knowing that God knows you better than you know yourself help you?

_____

_____

_____

→ **Respond**

Try to not get defensive when you feel misunderstood today. Believe the best about people by imagining they are trying their best. Realize that others are not as introspective as you and that their lack of questions doesn't necessarily mean they don't care.

10   Isa. 55:9

Day 11:

The Search for Significance

For he grew up before him like a young plant, and like a root out of dry ground;

he had no form or majesty that we should look at him, and no beauty that we

should desire him.

—Isaiah 53:2

"PEACOCKS ARE BEAUTIFUL, BUT THEIR BEHAVIOR IS not." The headline was too strange not to read further as the wildlife columnist described the troubles these bright creatures caused to their Bay Area neighborhood. The tag went hilariously on: "Danville peacocks are causing a ruckus, pooping everywhere and destroying gardens."[1] We have to wonder if the flamboyant birds had any idea of the disruption they caused, or if they were just happy to have a place to spread their wings and ... leave their mark.

> You have made us for yourself, O Lord, and our heart is restless until it rests in you.
>
> —St. Augustine

---

1   Joan Morris, "Peacocks Are Beautiful, but Their Behavior Is Not," The Mercury News, June 8, 2018, https://www.mercurynews.com/2018/06/08/peacocks-are-beautiful-but-their-behavior-is-not/.

Enneagram teacher Richard Rohr compares the "heart types" (Twos, Threes, and Fours) to a peacock:

> The peacock shows himself off. His getup draws attention to him. The long-term goal of counseling for heart types must be to bundle away the peacock and to dock his tail, so that it becomes clear that without his finery he is just as much a normal, ugly chicken as the rest of us.[2]

This humorous illustration describes the desire of the heart types to show off their impressive, glorious feathers. It's as though every act comes with a plea, "Please see my beautiful feathers; validate me, see me!" More specifically, Twos want to show off through their sacrifice, Threes through success, and Fours through uniqueness.

Fours chase uniqueness and originality through being attractive, creative, eccentric, extravagant, esoteric, or different. Sameness or ordinary are bad words. That is why Fours often intentionally stand in contrast to their surroundings. If others are wearing the same style, they change; if others are happy, they feel a draw towards sadness. Fours deep down truly do want to connect with others, but often fail when they give in to the impulse to be different at all times—when their belief of tortured individuality gets in the way of cohesive community.

> Jesus died on the cross for you—for your flawed and ordinary self, not your unique, special, crafted self.

Fours seek to craft a social persona that is fundamentally different or set apart from everyone else. It is difficult to accept that Someone we can neither see nor touch already sees us as significant, so we drift from the gospel's promise of unconditional love and work hard to project an image of unmatched uniqueness to those we can actually see and touch. We become master sculptors, crafting an image—exchanging the glory of God for the glory of man.[3] We pick up the chisel and begin carving the perfect persona for others to admire, handing over our God-given need for acceptance to people (ironically, those same people we try so

2   Rohr and Ebert, *The Enneagram*, 88.

3   Rom. 1:23

hard to be different from) rather than God. It's almost as if we want others to hear, "I am one of a kind; therefore, you can't abandon me."

Jesus "had no form or majesty that we should look at him, and no beauty that we should desire him,"[4] and yet, early in His ministry—before He accomplished anything newsworthy—the skies opened at His baptism and heard the affirming voice of the Father reminding Him just how valuable He is. We, too, in our baptism—this mystical moment of physicalizing the burial and resurrection of Christ—are reminded of our eternal acceptance. Just as a parent holds their newborn child in the delivery room in a gaze of sheer delight before they have done anything worthy of love, so too does the Father gaze at you, *exactly as you are.*

The Good News for Individualists is Jesus died on the cross for *you*—for your flawed and ordinary self, not your unique, special, crafted self. You are, simply by virtue of being God's child, a partaker in the *imago Dei*, a unique piece of art; no amount of chiseling on your part can change that. Just as every flower of the field may be similar and yet individually lovely, you too are strikingly unique and as beloved as every creature upon whom the divine light of love and acceptance shines.

→ Pray

Father, forgive me for looking in the mirror too much. I've served my image, not Yours. I spend so much of my day fixated on how others see me rather than how You see me. Cleanse my heart of every inclination to steal the glory You deserve so I can exchange it for human admiration. Remind me that Your Son's death is proof that I don't need to pursue any other acceptance than Yours, which You already gave.

---

4 Isa. 53:2b

Day 11 Reflections:

How do you feel driven to be noticeably different? What aspects of your image do you spend the most time sculpting?

_____

_____

_____

_____

In what ways might your life become more restful if you stopped the restless pursuit of standing out?

_____

_____

_____

_____

How did Jesus chase lasting significance? Where do you see growth in your life toward this end?

_____

_____

_____

_____

→ Respond

Write out all the reasons God loves you without listing any of your titles, special roles, or awards.

Day 12:

The Longing

For we know that the whole creation has been groaning together in the pains of childbirth until now. And not only the creation, but we ourselves, who have the firstfruits of the Spirit, groan inwardly as we wait eagerly for adoption as sons, the redemption of our bodies.

—Romans 8:22-23

ROCK AND ROLL LEGENDS U2 WERE ONCE members of a Christian fellowship called *Shalom*. As the band became more well-known, they wondered if they should be doing something "more meaningful." According to the understandings of the day, rock and roll seemed at odds with their Christian faith. But their manager pressured them to stick with it—and well, the rest is history. U2's hit song "I Still Haven't Found What I'm Looking For" was released in 1987 and Bono referred to it as "a gospel song with a restless spirit."[2]

I yearn, therefore I am.

—Marc Gafni[1]

For Fours who grew up in a Christian subculture that only stresses the positive,

---

1 Marc Gafni, *The Mystery of Love* (United Kingdom: Atria Books, 2004), 36.

2 Elizabeth Blair, "In U2's 'I Still Haven't Found What I'm Looking For,' A Restless Search For Meaning," NPR, July 26, 2019, https://www.npr.org/2019/07/26/743620996/u2-i-still-havent-found-what-im-looking-for-american-anthem.

this hit song is an anthem of understood longing. Fans stretching across generations and continents have resonated with it's authentic message because it taps into our *real* life experiences: the doubting, disappointments, waiting, wanting, and searching.

The Individualist's life has been likened to a search for the Holy Grail.[3] Movies like *Monty Python and the Holy Grail* (1975), *Indiana Jones and the Last Crusade* (1989), or Thomas Mallory's *La Morte d'Arthur* (for the real nerds) are fictional accounts that have tried to capture the lofty quests of archeologists and historians to recover this ancient, eternal life-bestowing artifact.[4] Today, as a result, the term Holy Grail represents something that you want very much, something that could change everything if only it were obtained, but is impossible to find. Do you know the feeling?

> On this journey, we open our hands and let go of what might have been or what could be to receive more of Him.

Do you find yourself playing the "if only" game? For the Four, it almost seems too effortless to spot someone with a more interesting and satisfying life than them. "*If* I had their upbringing, job, education, style, or talent *then* I would be content." Strangely enough, one of the reasons Fours strive for the unattainable is because they actually *enjoy* the longing—even if (sometimes *because*) it's unachievable. Fours generally are disappointed when they finally possess the object of their desire, often coming to see it as a counterfeit. But you don't have to feel bad about that; never apologize for your longings. As I watch you yearn for things to be on earth as they are in heaven, I feel myself being pulled into the deeper terrain of my own desires. You are a gift to me.

Pay attention this week to how your *longing* affects your *be-longing*. Drew Moser, author of *The Enneagram of Discernment*, insightfully shared: "Longing is directed toward that which is beyond our grasp. Belonging is experienced in that which

---

3   Wagner, *Nine Lenses*, 268.

4   "Holy Grail," History.com, June 7, 2019, https://www.history.com/topics/middle-ages/holy-grail.

is in our midst."[5] In other words, too much longing for what we cannot achieve will keep us from belonging in the present. Too much nostalgia (clinging to past events, lovers, or suffering) or idealism (clinging to extraordinary, fanciful, future dreams) may actually enlarge the gap between you and others—reinforcing the feeling that you don't belong. Therefore, catch yourself when your mind starts wandering and strive to be present with others. Resist the temptation to always be set apart; embrace the ordinary and observe how it increases your sense of belonging.

The Good News for Individualists is that God is with us in the longing. Longing is not an end, but it's the path we travel *with* God. On this journey we open our hands and let go of what might have been or what could be to receive more of Him. He wants to know you even when you are withdrawn and engulfed in restless longings. In Him, you have someone to long with.

If you find your mind searching today, remember that a Savior came searching for you. As Jessica Kantrowitz wrote, "In my own body, the depths of me, somewhere between my abdomen and my belly, was a sanctuary I'd never imagined."[6] In her battle with depression, she was reminded that her "body is a temple of the Holy Spirit"[7] and that God is always present. Remember, you are not alone. The Spirit, with all of creation, is groaning with you today.

→ Pray

Father, I will delight myself in You today. I know that eventually You will fulfill the desires of my heart in this life and in the life to come. My heart groans today because things are not as they ought to be in the world. Open my eyes to see You walking with me and holding my dreams, doubts, and disappointments as we await the new creation together.

---

5   Drew Moser, *The Enneagram of Discernment: The Way of Vocation, Wisdom, and Practice* (Beaver Falls, PA: Falls City Press, 2020), 206.

6   Jessica Kantrowitz, *The Long Night: Readings and Stories to Help You Through Depression* (United States: Fortress Press, 2020), 38-39.

7   1 Cor. 6:19

Day 12 Reflections:

What are you longing for today? What prayers are you waiting for God to answer?

_____

_____

_____

_____

How does focusing on your differences with others affect your connectedness to them? What can you do to close the gap?

_____

_____

_____

_____

What might change if you truly believed your body was a sanctuary where the Spirit of God dwells?

_____

_____

_____

_____

→ Respond

Put your hand out in front of your face. Say, "The Lord is at hand" to remind yourself of how close God is to you. Using the words of the Psalmist, say out loud, "Your face, LORD, do I seek." No matter the state of your heart today, remind your soul that "He will take you in."[8]

---

8 Ps. 27:8-10

Day 13:

Addicted to Love

Set me as a seal upon your heart, as a seal upon your arm, for love is strong as

death, jealousy is fierce as the grave. Its flashes are flashes of fire, the very flame

of the LORD. Many waters cannot quench love, neither can floods drown it. If a

man offered for love all the wealth of his house, he would be utterly despised.

—Song of Solomon 8:6-7

I HAVE A CONFESSION TO MAKE: I'VE made a lot of mistakes in the relationship department. After ending a deep two-plus year relationship, with a big void in my heart to fill, I immediately began pursuing another girl. I went all out with this rebound: even buying a journal with an Eiffel Tower on it (she loved Paris), in which I wrote daily, chronicling every detail of our first weeks together. But after four months, I didn't feel the same about the relationship. What once was so fresh and new had suddenly lost my interest. I began to push her away, offering the classic line, "It's not you; it's me." Her face turned deathly cold and she said, "I have

> Might as well face it, you're addicted to love.
>
> –Robert Palmer[1]

1 "Addicted to Love," Lyrics.com, accessed on May 13, 2021, https://www.lyrics.com/lyric/2828967/Robert+Palmer/Addicted+To+Love.

dated other guys who were complete jerks. But you are the worst of them all—because you led me on and made me believe you loved me."

My friend once told me I was "in love with being in love." I thought he was crazy. Have you been told that? Naranjo explains why Fours are often called The Romantics:

"Love must and does appear as the ticket to paradise, where all woe ends: no more loneliness, no more feeling lost, guilty or unworthy; no more responsibility for self; no more struggle with a harsh world for which he feels hopelessly unequipped. Instead love seems to promise protection, support, affection, encouragement, sympathy, understanding. It will give him a feeling of worth, it will give meaning to his life, it will be salvation and redemption."[2]

Fours love nothing more than chasing after the imaginary fire of perfect love and intimacy and others unfortunately get burned by the pursuit. As Helen Palmer says, "There's juice in the longing."[3] We easily become infatuated, leading to fantasies of many kinds: the sky is full of relational castles we began construction on, only to abandon.

More than any lover, friend, or family, longing is the Four's most intimate, lifelong companion.

Aside from the potential partners who are left in the rubble, such single-minded pursuit of imaginary soul mates into whom we can pour our whole selves often ends with a disregard of family and friends. The result can be a long list of lost relationships—romantic *and* platonic; people who were once intimate parts of our lives, but who were abandoned (or maneuvered to abandon us) when reality caught up to the fantasy. Sometimes, this list of past lovers (and friends) is not easy to let go, and Fours' defensive mechanism of *introjection* means they may adopt the lost person(s) into their psyche and continually mourn them in order

2 Naranjo, *Character and Neurosis*, 116.

3 Palmer, *The Enneagram in Love and Work*, 114.

to stay in a state of perpetual yearning.[4] This may appear torturous, but the underlying need is to keep the lost person close to them so that they don't have to say goodbye and feel abandoned.[5] Remember, more than any lover, friend, or family, *longing* is the Four's most intimate, lifelong companion.

As she sings in our passage today, the maiden in Song of Solomon pleads with her beloved to seal her upon his heart, making the relationship permanent. She then proclaims that her feelings are like an unquenchable flame with a power as strong as death. If anything tries to come between her and her beloved, it will be met with a ferocious jealousy—the desire to keep what is rightfully hers. Her words are poetic and powerful, bearing much of the same heart-gripping imaginative power as your own creative energies.

But her words are not merely artfully expressive, they are full of deep wisdom. This hopeless romantic gives us some advice from personal experience: "Do not stir up or awaken love until it pleases."[6] Why not? Love is a fire—the most powerful force known to humanity. Love is capable of launching wars, of sustaining partners through decades of difficulty … or of saving all people through a life and act of self-sacrifice.

The Good News for Individualists is found in John 4, where we read about another woman, perpetually searching for true love and security, who meets Jesus by a well. Though the search has left her emotionally and physically empty and distant from all others in her community, this Rescuer lovingly offers an eternally fulfilling relationship. With the eyes of loving-kindness, He offers her an eternal spring of intimate fulfillment that no partner could fulfill. I know it's difficult to maintain relationships when what's in your head doesn't match reality, but the transforming love of Christ offers a grounding in the people and this world as it is—He offers us a path to loving the reality He came to save, not merely our imaginings. Don't let your longings keep you from enjoying your committed relationships; focus on what they can become, not what they are.

---

4   *Introjection*: the unconscious adoption of the ideas or attitudes of others.

5   Wagner, *Nine Lenses*, 280.

6   Song of Sol. 2:7; 3:5; 8:4

> ### → Pray
>
> Father, You are a spring of living water overflowing in my heart. No matter what happens in my earthly relationships, I know You will never leave me. You see the depths of my sin and yet want to draw closer still. Thank You for giving me the ability to dream. Now, help me to have realistic expectations so that I can show others the same commitment You've shown me.

Day 13 Reflections:

When have you been "addicted to love?"

_____

_____

_____

_____

How has your romanticism or idealism served you well in your work or relationships?

_____

_____

_____

Who from your past have you not fully grieved or let go of?

_____

_____

_____

> ### → Respond
>
> Write a goodbye letter to someone from your past to get closure. Include why you are saying goodbye, how it makes you feel, special memories with them, things they taught you, what you want them to know, and what you will always remember.[7]

---

7   This exercise comes from www.therapistaid.com.

Day 14:

The Happiness of Being Sad

My soul also is greatly troubled. But you, O Lord—how long? ... I am weary

with my moaning; every night I flood my bed with tears; I drench my couch

with my weeping.

—Psalm 6:3,6

I'VE ALWAYS LOVED SONGS IN MINOR KEYS—THEIR plangent, darker notes have a way of playing with my heart, of opening space within me that brighter tones simply cannot. In general, people characterize the major keys as "happy," while the minors are "sad." Major music is used in celebrations, such as Mendelssohn's "Wedding March," or the traditional "Happy Birthday" tune. However, minor music is used for mourning and contemplation, such as Chopin's "Funeral March" or John Williams' "Schindler's List" soundtrack.

> Melancholy is the happiness of being sad.
>
> –Victor Hugo[1]

Music psychologist Glen Schellenberg analyzed more than 1,000 songs from 1965 to 2009. In 1965, every one of the *Billboard* Top 40 songs were in a major key, but over the next few decades, the tide began to turn: by 2009, only 18 of the Top 40 songs

---

1   Cron and Stabile, *The Road Back to You*, 153.

were in a major key. Schellenberg concluded, "People have come to appreciate sadness and ambiguity more. Life is more complicated, and they want the things that they consume as pleasure to be complex similarly."[2]

Do you appreciate sad books, movies, or songs? Do tragic tales strike deep within you? You may even experience life's disappointments as somewhat comforting, finding consistently positive people annoying or even deluded. When healthy, you are bearing witness to something the world's incorrigible optimists are still learning: "Sunshine all the time makes a desert."[3] Knowing very well the limitations of staying on the bright side, Fours embrace the valleys of life because they know the darkness can lead us more deeply into the heart of life. Only through grief can we grow strong roots—true transformation comes through great love and great suffering, attests Richard Rohr.[4] In the parable of the sower, the seed sown on rocky soil represents someone who sprouts quickly with great excitement, but dies when trouble comes because they don't have the deep roots to sustain them. Truly, the seed must be allowed to be buried in death in order to sprout new life.[5]

> Your life—who you are—is a minor key that must be played for the world.

Many of the Psalms (about 40 percent) were written in a "minor key," in the language of *lament*—which is why I avoided the book for so long. In fact, the Psalms were my least favorite book of the Bible. (Don't hate me, I'm just being authentic!) They felt too emotionally volatile and often even seemed written specifically for more "needy types." The broader Christian subculture seems to agree with where I was for so long. In comparison with the movement on the secular *Billboard* charts, only 5-10 percent of the top 100 contemporary worship songs could be argued as lament songs, as Soong-Chan Rah, author of *Prophetic Lament*, says.

---

2   "Why We're Happy Being Sad: Pop's Emotional Evolution," NPR, September 4, 2012, https://www.npr.org/2012/09/04/160548025/why-were-happy-being-sad-pops-emotional-evolution.

3   Arab proverb.

4   Richard Rohr, *The Universal Christ: How a Forgotten Reality Can Change Everything We See, Hope For, and Believe* (Crown Publishing Group: 2019), 83.

5   Matt. 13:20-21; John 12:24-26

This was my lifelong posture until my naivety and stoicism were shattered through suffering and there was very little left of this false self. In the aftermath of that difficult season, I spent a full year only reading and memorizing from the Psalms. The laments, in particular, have taken deep root in my soul and are still bearing fruit.[6]

Martin Luther said of the Psalms, "When they speak of fear and hope, they use such words that no painter could so depict for your fear or hope, and no Cicero or other orator so portray them. And that they speak these words to God and with God, this, I repeat, is the best thing of all."[7] For anyone who has felt pain too deep for words over sin, sickness, persecution, bullying, or some other kind of suffering, these ancient hymns bring healing through one of the most powerful phrases in the human vocabulary: *me too.*

Our hype-filled, achieving, pragmatic world needs your gift of lament now more than ever. We need you to hold our hands and walk with us through these darkened valleys with which you are so familiar. Your life—who you are—is a minor key that must be played for the world. Within you is a reservoir of resources that can take us collectively deeper and and more authentically down the path of Christ.

The Good News for Individualists is that we worship the God who "became flesh and blood, and moved into the neighborhood."[8] We follow the One who is familiar with suffering, not intellectually, but through personal, lived experience. The Psalmist, wiping away his tears, assures himself, "The LORD has heard my plea; the LORD accepts my prayer."[9] Though Jesus' disciples in the garden of Gethsemane kept falling asleep as He sweats tears of blood in agony, be assured that Jesus stays awake with you in your grieving. The Man of Sorrows who lamented over Jerusalem gives you permission to lament as well.[10]

---

6   Soong-Chan Rah, "Prophetic Lament: A Call for Justice, Love, and Humility in Troubled Times," Biola University Center for Christian Thought, June 15, 2017, https://cct.biola.edu/prophetic-lament-call-justice-love-humility-troubled-times/.

7   Timothy J. Wengert, *Word of Life: Introducing Lutheran Hermeneutics* (United States: Fortress Press, 2019), 127.

8   John 1:14 MSG

9   Ps. 6:9

10   Matt. 23:37-39

→ Pray

Father, You are the God of all comfort who hears my cries. Do not let me grieve without hope like the rest of the world, but finish every song of lament with confidence in Your abiding presence. Give me the courage to teach the world a different tune—one that allows others to be comforted by the music of the gospel in every high and every low.

Day 14 Reflections:

How is melancholy a sweet sadness for you?

_____

_____

_____

_____

Do you feel you've been given permission to lament?

_____

_____

_____

_____

What is one thing you can do to help your family or church learn how to lament?

_____

_____

_____

_____

→ Respond

Write out your own prayer of lament using Psalm 22. What are you feeling (vv. 1-2)? What has been the most difficult part of the struggle? What do you want the Lord to do (vv. 19-21)? What praises will you proclaim (vv. 22-31)?

Day 15:

The Push-Pull Dance

Then Saul said, "I have sinned. Return, my son David, for I will no more do you

harm, because my life was precious in your eyes this day. Behold, I have acted

foolishly, and have made a great mistake."

—1 Samuel 26:21

AS WE'VE DISCUSSED, FOURS EXIST IN A state of perpetual longing, yet that does not remove the desire to obtain the object of our longing. However, once we've finally gained what was sought, how long until it has lost its luster? How long until the thing or person that was supposed to fill our desire is proven unequal to the task? Then what do we do? Do you often find yourself *pushing* others away when they "lose their shine," only to *pull* them back after they feel out of reach? One of the hallmark features of Individualists is this "push-pull" dance. A Four

> **Go away but don't leave.**
>
> –Suzanne Stabile[1]

says, "If you take a step forward, I take a step back. If you take a step back, I take a step toward you."[2]

---

1 Stabile, *The Path Between Us*, 110.

2 Rohr and Ebert, *The Enneagram*, 105.

Friends and family consistently point to this "dance" as one of the most challenging aspects of being in relationship with Fours. Suzzane Stabile says the conflicting message Fours sometimes put out to others is: "Go away, but don't leave."[3] They can behave like a cat who purrs in your lap one moment, only to scratch your face the next. Unhealthy Fours may play an ongoing game of hide and seek—testing others to see if they will pursue them when they are at their worst. They play "hard to get" to see if others will notice and come to their rescue.

At their worst, Fours will *push* by creating a little more drama (the "making up" will be that much sweeter), and may even express elements of codependency, clinging to relationships that are frustrating precisely because emotional intensity is their juice. But many people have a much lower tolerance for this seemingly manipulative dance—particularly the stronger, self-possessed people with whom Fours often enter relationships. This push-pull behavior can feel like "emotional blackmail"[4] and drive away these sought-after rescuers for good, creating a cycle of prophesied abandonment, followed by unconscious self-fulfillment.

> God always pulls us close, never pushing us away when we are caught naked and exposed.

King Saul, who we dealt with in the *Spears of Envy* devotion, displayed a similar push-pull behavior with David. When Saul was tormented by a harmful spirit, he employed David to play the lyre for him to soothe his tortured soul. Pulling the young man still closer, Saul made him his personal armor bearer and encouraged David's friendship with the prince, Jonathon.[5] After David's legendary defeat of Goliath, the people have a new hero to fall in love with and sing praises of, and Saul naturally feels envious of this attention (especially considering that the people name him as inferior in their songs of David). In the end, Saul pushes David away by literally throwing spears at him.[6] This pattern continues throughout

---

3   Stabile, *The Path Between Us*, 110.

4   Claudio Naranjo, *The Enneagram of Society: Healing the Soul to Heal the World* (United States: Gateways Books & Tapes, 2004), 128.

5   1 Sam. 16:14-23

6   1 Sam. 18-19

their relationship, with David remaining consistently loyal to the king, while Saul could not decide whether to embrace his servant as a son or stab him as a traitor.

To be clear, I'm not saying Saul was a Four—and very few people of any number express such clearly destructive behavior—but this exaggerated example may help us see some of the potential pitfalls for the Individualist in unhealthy spaces.

The Good News for Individualists is that God always pulls us close, never pushing us away when we are caught naked and exposed.. As with Adam and Eve, He makes the sacrifice to cover us, reaching out to touch and heal us like the leper. Like the woman caught in adultery, He advocates on our behalf, forgiving our denials of His love, and redeeming us at our worst like the thief on the cross. How good it is to worship a God who doesn't stir up drama or play games with our hearts. You don't have to wonder how God feels about you today—He hasn't changed His mind about you, for "Jesus Christ is the same yesterday and today and forever."[7]

→ Pray

Father, Your unending mercies are new every morning, and Your love never ceases toward me.[8] Help me to draw others close and keep them close. When I feel like pushing others away, fill me with the same loyal, steadfast love You've given me. Enable me to unceasingly forgive those who have intentionally or unintentionally shamed me.

---

7   Heb. 13:8

8   Lam. 3:22-23

Day 15 Reflections:

How have you noticed yourself doing the push-pull dance?

_____

_____

_____

_____

What forms of sulking do you display when you are unhappy? What behavior are you trying to elicit from others?

_____

_____

_____

_____

When have you displayed steadfast love rather than pushing someone away?

_____

_____

_____

_____

→ Respond

Try to "catch yourself in the act" today of focusing on what's off in a relationship. Notice if there is a tendency to ignore all of the good aspects of the relationship and "throw the baby out with the bath water" by pulling away.

Day 16:

Finding Equanimity

... so that we may no longer be children, tossed to and fro by the waves and carried about by every wind of doctrine, by human cunning, by craftiness in deceitful schemes.

—Ephesians 4:14

THERE WAS ONCE A YOUNG MAN TORMENTED by a red lizard sitting on his shoulder—he hated this vile little beast, yet also found he could not imagine life without it. An angel came along and promised to kill it, and the man was happy. Happy, that is, until the angel began glowing with a fiery heat and he realized just how painful this experience would be. Over time, the attached lizard had almost become a part of him, and he wondered if its death would lead to his as well. After some hesitation, the lizard was finally killed and a stallion emerged from where it fell. The newly freed man rode off in joy on this great steed into heaven.

> More than once in life I've had to say to myself, I am not my feelings.
>
> –Ian Cron[1]

---

1   Cron and Stabile, *The Road Back to You*, 165.

This lizard, found in C.S. Lewis's *The Great Divorce*, represents an outward manifestation of the man's lust and inner battle to be freed from it. I believe this illustration can also serve as a metaphor for the Individualist's turbulent relationship with their feelings. Feelings can be a controlling, all-consuming, even enslaving force—something that simultaneously tortures and ... seems to complete you. Simply put, feelings make you, you. When understood and valued properly, feelings can become like a stallion under your control, leading you higher and farther on the journey.

The Four's *virtue*, which is a quality of the heart experienced when you are abiding in God, is said to be *equanimity*. Equanimity literally means "an equal mind."[2] When your mind is balanced, you can feel your feelings

> You are no longer a slave but a steward of your emotions.

without being consumed by them. Like the young man in Lewis's story, you can let go without feeling like you are losing yourself. Equanimity allows you to feel fully alive in the calm of life, rather than having to stir up intense emotions. Composed and steady, you can view your emotions as separate from you—as swirling, temporary clouds moving around the solid mountain. Treat them like dinner guests. Learn what you can from them and spend sufficient time trying to experience and understand them, but don't invite them to stay the night.

The apostle Paul asked his followers in Ephesus to imagine themselves as ships on the sea being dashed by the surging waves. These powerful external forces are likened to deceitful influences that wreak havoc on those who are unanchored. While Paul put a particular emphasis on the danger of false doctrine, I think you can also use this metaphor to describe the deceitfulness of raging emotions, throwing us off course and in danger of shipwreck.

When we are carried along by the Holy Spirit—the presence of Christ within all things—rather than our emotions, we will find our equilibrium. We will respond to others from the balanced soul of people knowing who and whose they are. No longer needing to be overdramatic, envious, correct, or unique, we will respond

---

2 Chestnut, *The Complete Enneagram*, 307.

to our circumstances with a level of emotion that the specific situation calls for, leaving us prepared to offer the healing presence only a balanced Four can.

The Good News for Individualists is that God is a safer refuge than your emotions. As the Psalmist sings, "God is our refuge and strength, a very present help in trouble. Therefore we will not fear though the earth gives way, though the mountains be moved into the heart of the sea, though its waters roar and foam, though the mountains tremble at its swelling."[3] When you are caught in the whirlwind of emotions this week, picture yourself on the boat with the disciples in the middle of the storm. Rather than running around frantic, imagine yourself sitting next to Jesus while He's asleep in the stern. Close your eyes and let the winds pass over, knowing that the God of peace who is present in the storm will soon say, "Be still."[4]

Be encouraged that God sees your emotions as valid and important. Though others may be dismissive of the way you feel or shame you for being "too emotional," God uses them to help you better understand yourself and others. After all, emotions are a gift from Him. Just remember that your emotions are a *gauge*, not a *guide*. If your feelings become your GPS, you are bound to get lost. Let the Word of God, Holy Spirit, and community of faith be your guide. As a child of God, remember that you are no longer a *slave* but a *steward* of your emotions—to use for His redemptive purposes.

→ Pray

Father, thank You for allowing me to feel things deeply. While others tolerate my emotions, You are fascinated by them. Thank You for sending Jesus to free me from being enslaved to my emotions and from using them in all the wrong ways. Sometimes, I feel very lost and disillusioned in this world. Guide me with Your Spirit so that I feel safe and secure.

---

3   Ps. 46:1-3

4   Mark. 4:38-40

Day 16 Reflections:

How do you use your emotions to influence others in a positive way?

_____

_____

_____

_____

Why is it hard to let go of your emotions, rise above them, or respond to a situation with balance?

_____

_____

_____

_____

What can you do to honor your emotions without allowing them to be your guide?

_____

_____

_____

_____

➜ Respond

When you feel overwhelmed by a very strong emotion today, practice the discipline of waiting. Instead of overindulging, over-responding, or over-identifying with the emotion, wait for it to pass. Then, ask yourself what you can learn from this and what God wants you to do about it.

Day 17:

Stress Triggers

And Moses lifted up his hand and struck the rock with his staff twice, and water

came out abundantly, and the congregation drank, and their livestock. And the

LORD said to Moses and Aaron, "Because you did not believe in me, to uphold

me as holy in the eyes of the people of Israel, therefore you shall not bring this

assembly into the land that I have given them."

—Numbers 20:11-12

WE ALL GET STRESSED FROM TIME TO time, but if we don't pay attention to the warning signs, we will find ourselves at the breaking point quickly—maybe even in the midst of a public meltdown. Beatrice Chestnut shares some of the most common triggers for the Individualist in her book, *The 9 Types of Leadership:*[2]

• When people can't slow down long enough to get to know me.

No pressure, no diamonds.

–Thomas Carlyle[1]

• When people don't value my contribution or appreciate the work I do.

---

1   Iam A. Freeman, *Seeds of Revolution: A Collection of Axioms, Passages and Proverbs, Volume 1* (United Kingdom: iUniverse, 2014), 74.

2   Chestnut, *The 9 Types of Leadership*, 307.

- When people perceive me as negative or pessimistic when I am trying to help by bringing attention to what is missing.

- When people don't understand what I am saying or how I am feeling but keep insisting that they do.

- When others prioritize speed and efficiency over getting the aesthetics right.

- When my bosses make me spend a lot of time working on mundane tasks that don't have meaning to me.

- When people tell me to "just get over it" or "look on the bright side" when I am having difficult feelings about what's going on.

Fours are most comfortable in the uncomfortable extremes, often even experiencing both ends of the emotional spectrum multiple times within a short time. This internal back and forth often leads to explosions caused by either extreme highs *or* lows. For instance, a stressed or bored Four may become irritated with the smallest of difficulties, becoming extremely verbal (and often sarcastic), or withdraw into themselves and push others away. They may become workaholics or aggressively competitive, trying to prove themselves in extreme ways or go to the opposite extreme, wallowing in feelings of helpless inadequacy. Under severe pressure, Fours may play the role of a martyr or become vindictive if someone has deflated their self-esteem and made them feel insignificant.

> Let your stress lead to sanctification—a cleansing.

The Bible presents many case studies of people who displayed life's extreme emotions, and shut down completely or lashed out in a public meltdown because of stress. One of those whose failure was very visible (and came with steep consequences) is Moses. More than once, he seems to throw up his hands, telling God he would rather die than deal with the Israelites another moment; however, there are other moments when it appears to be only Moses standing between God's wrath and the disobedient nation. While the shutdowns often occur in private, Moses' public meltdowns occur in front of the entire nation—like the one at Meribah, when he strikes the rock.[3]

Moses had a very stressful job—in the hot desert for over 40 years, no less! It's certainly understandable that he sometimes bends past the breaking point. He listens to constant complaining, bickering, and backsliding and is somehow supposed to always know what to do. Not only that, but his leadership and authority are also under constant threat by his own friends and family. We hear often of Moses' self-doubt, frustration, loneliness, and anger, and his final public failure at Meribah is the stated reason he is denied entry to the promised land. Nonetheless, Moses always recovers and stands with his people, leading them to the doorstep of Canaan.

The Good News for Individualists is that there is a way to bend without breaking. With proper care for your mental health and trusted relationships with those to whom you have given permission to call you out before you break down, you can both preserve your reputation and "uphold [God] as holy in the eyes of the people."[4] Just as the apostle Paul told his spiritual children that he was in the "anguish of childbirth" until Christ was formed in them, so too is your heavenly Father toiling to finish the work He began in you.[5]

Let your stress lead to sanctification—a cleansing. Jesus' work on the cross was a receiving of the world's extremes and a reverberation of compassion and love. With Jesus' help, your suffering and stress can be what lead you to experience (and give) grace in the midst of the whirlwind, creating in you greater empathy and compassion toward even the most insensitive or dismissive people you know.

→ Pray

Father, thank You for sending Your Son to be our example of someone who bent without breaking. Through opposition, persecution, and even death, He did not fold. Oh Lord, let the same compassion flow out of me that flowed out of Jesus after He was struck on the cross. With Your steadfast patience, help me point my friends and enemies to the promised land of a life lived with You today.

---

3 Num. 20:10-13

4 Num. 20:12

5 Gal. 4:19; Phil. 1:6

Day 17 Reflections:

What triggers your stress most often? Which extreme do you tend to gravitate toward in stress?

_____

_____

_____

_____

Who are the people in your life monitoring your "meltdown meter?"

_____

_____

_____

_____

How does looking to Jesus on the cross change the way you respond to stress?

_____

_____

_____

_____

➜ Respond

The next time you feel stressed, ask yourself: "Am I Hungry, Angry, Lonely, or Tired?" This H. A. L. T. acronym serves as a reminder that our stress is often a result of our basic needs not getting met.

Day 18:
Dramatic or Melodramatic

His eyes are like a flame of fire, and on his head are many diadems ... He is
clothed in a robe dipped in blood, and the name by which he is called is The
Word of God. ... From his mouth comes a sharp sword with which to strike
down the nations, and he will rule them with a rod of iron. He will tread the
winepress of the fury of the wrath of God the Almighty.

—Revelation 19:12-15

YOU MIGHT HAVE NOTICED THAT THE BIBLE has a flair for the dramatic. The apostle John's Revelation, in particular, resembles a Marvel movie with fiery-eyed Jesus wearing a bloody robe and descending from the sky with full pyrotechnics and a sword coming out of His mouth. In this book we also encounter the four horsemen, locusts with human faces, and a multi-headed, horned beast coming up out of the water. There's nothing ordinary about it.

> If no one answers the
> phone, dial louder.
>
> –Lucy van Pelt, Peanuts

Jesus, like John after and the prophets before Him, wasn't afraid of dramatizing His language to make a point: "Truly, truly, I say to you, unless you eat the flesh of the Son of Man and drink his blood, you have no life in you."[1] When speaking about the fate of Jerusalem or the world, Jesus borrowed theatrical images from the Hebrew Scriptures: "... the sun will be darkened, and the moon will not give its light, and the stars will fall from heaven ... ."[2] Jesus also healed people by putting His fingers in ears, spitting and touching tongues, rubbing mud in eyes, and exorcising demons into a herd of pigs.

Doing things out of the ordinary to make a point is a useful skill in helping others to see the reality of a situation and respond appropriately to God's wonder and warnings. Your vibrant language and impassioned works put an exclamation on our lived experience, but problems arise when the Individualist moves from being dramatic to *melodramatic*. Look no further than the prophet Jonah, who bemoaned the withering of a shade plant more desperately than the impending doom of the Ninevites. My friend Jesse Eubanks told me Jonah missed an opportunity here to lean into the growth arrow of the Four (Type One) by pursuing righteousness, justice, and trusting obedience to God. Instead, shaking his fist at God, Jonah announced he was "angry enough to die."[3] Similarly, Fours under the deepest distress may sigh deeply over their plight and lament their victimhood to others.

> Fictional, exaggerated, and unrealistic melodramas are perfect for the big screen, but not when a Four's life actually becomes one.

Fictional, exaggerated, and unrealistic melodramas are perfect for the big screen, but not when a Four's life actually becomes one. This stirring up of life's drama fulfills an inner need to intensify life: Fours may select an album, piece of art, or another object in order to adrenalize their mood of choice. Because identity gets tied to feelings, the aesthetics and atmosphere become tools to reinforce a sense of self.[4]

---

1   John 6:53

2   Matt. 24:29

3   Jonah 4:9

4   Riso and Hudson, *Personality Types*, 150.

Ian Cron adds, "Fours are intense. They want to dig down to the heart to deal with whatever's going on between you and them. If they're on an emotional mountaintop, they want you to be there with them, and if they're feeling low and morbidly self-interested, they might invite you over so they can share their woes over a bottle of wine in the hope that you can fix them. Fours can leverage trivial events or situations into opportunities to show off their Shakespearean flair."[5]

Because of this flair for the overly dramatic, one area of growth is to try and "catch yourself" when emotions are amping up in order to avoid feeling empty or to keep your relationships from feeling dull. Pay attention to when you let your imagination turn into a melodrama and watch how you might "color outside the lines" of reality and put expressions on peoples' faces or words in their mouths that aren't true. Resist the temptation to overshare just to raise the authenticity bar to a height that no one else can match—though occasionally this can lead to deepening trust and affection, it often causes people to lean *back* rather than forward.[6] Make sure to go to God first since He has the capacity to handle your strong emotions and heal your full self—much as the prophets, the psalmists, and Jesus Himself did. Express the fullness of your interior life to God in whatever way best encapsulates your state, and then bring the "revised draft" to your relationships. This will lower the stakes of your conversations, allowing others to respond in the ways you are hoping for.

The Good News for Individualists is that though God acts in dramatic ways He does not cease to be God in the calm. Standing on Mount Horeb, the prophet Elijah witnessed a strong wind break the rocks into pieces—but the Lord was not in the wind. Then he felt a strong earthquake, but the Lord was not in it either. Then, he saw a powerful fire appear but the Lord was not in it. Finally, in the calm after such a storm, the Lord appeared in the form of a small, quiet whisper.[7] With that image impressed in your mind today, find Him in the calm. Quiet your heart and let Him lead you beside still waters.[8]

---

5 Cron and Stabile, *The Road Back to You*, 159-160.

6 Stabile, *The Path Between Us*, 116.

7 1 Kings 19:9-18

8 Ps. 23:2

→ Pray

Father, I praise You for not being emotionally absent but full of life, wonder, and awe. I'm grateful for how You've called me to express Your truths in mysterious and profound ways. Help me to express the fullness of myself to You, and then allow You to lead me beside still waters.

Day 18 Reflections:

What is one of your favorite dramatic sayings or scenes from the Bible? What purpose does it serve?

_____

_____

_____

When have you done something out of the ordinary to make a statement? How did God use it for His purposes?

_____

_____

_____

How do you amp up your feelings in your imagination or through your physical environment to feel more alive?

_____

_____

_____

→ Respond

Identify someone who has made you feel angry or ashamed. Describe what you are feeling inside. Now, test your feelings by writing out evidence of things they've said or done to justify your feelings. Remember, feelings are not facts.

Day 19:

Fighting for Immunity

The next day he saw Jesus coming toward him, and said, "Behold, the Lamb of God, who takes away the sin of the world!

—John 1:29

IT'S EASY TO SEE THAT THE HUMAN body is the apex of God's creation—a marvelous machine of interconnected parts and systems working in concert to uphold a person as they walk through life. Our immune system for example is one vital part of the body, guarding against bacteria and viruses. When it senses these foreign intruders, it deploys fighter cells to attack the invaders. When the immune system is healthy, it can discern the difference between native and foreign cells. However, if you have an autoimmune disease, your body is deceived into thinking that the good parts of you are "the enemy."

> You are your own worst enemy. If you can learn to stop expecting impossible perfection, in yourself and others, you may find the happiness that has always eluded you.
>
> –Lisa Kleypas[1]

1   Lisa Kleypas, *Love in the Afternoon* (United States: St. Martin's Press, 2010), 321.

In this scenario, autoantibodies are again deployed, not to fight the true infection this time, but rather innocent cells—causing the person to attack themselves from within.[2] Applying this medical analogy to psychology, Naranjo said that the primary defense mechanism of Individualists, *introjection*, causes a similar "turning against the self."[3]

One of my favorite films of all time, *Inception*, concerns the use of futuristic dream-sharing technology to implant an idea into another person's mind as they are under a drug-induced sleep. When the dangerous task of "inception" is achieved, the target will awake believing it was their own natural experience and idea. This concept of "inception" becomes all too real for the Four when they adopt perceived negativity from another into their own psyche and come to deeply believe it themselves. For example, if a parent tells a child "You are dumb"—or if they even think the parent feels this way—the child may grow up telling themselves, "I am dumb."

> Jesus offers to remove the scarring words and shame-inducing attitudes of others that we've brought into our depths.

My sons and I take frequent trips to the children's museum here in Omaha. One of my son, Zeke's, favorite activities is the mining station. He pours a bag of sand and rocks into the pan and shakes it out until all of the sand is dumped into the stream underneath, leaving only the precious rocks behind. We all receive a mixed bag of encouragement and criticism every day, but sadly for a Four, the encouragement often falls through the cracks, leaving them with only a bag of rocks. The human brain is generally biased toward negative thoughts, but as with many aspects of the Individualist's life, this trait appears to be turned to eleven.

Ginger Lapid-Bogda explains, "Fours introject negative information—and repel positive data—about themselves as a way of coping with painful information and neutralizing external threats. They prefer to deal with self-inflicted damage

---

2   Stephanie Watson, "Autoimmune Diseases: Types, Symptoms, Causes, and More," Healthline, March 26, 2019, https://www.healthline.com/health/autoimmune-disorders.

3   Naranjo, *Character and Neurosis*, 125.

rather than having to respond to criticism or rejection from others."[4] In other words, turning against oneself through self-criticism is more tolerable than others' criticism—the epitome of "the devil you know" adage. On Mondays, when we evaluate my sermon, I often catch myself trying to beat others to the punch by verbalizing my failures before they get the chance. I'll even interrupt others' positive feedback because I know the negative is on the way, and I'd prefer it to come from *my* lips rather than theirs, allowing me to stay in control rather than become a victim.

The Good News for Individualists is that Jesus offers to remove the scarring words and shame-inducing attitudes of others that we've brought into our depths, resulting in feelings of self-rejection, abandonment, and insignificance. In ancient Israel, on the Day of Atonement, the high priest would place his hands on the head of a goat and confess the sins of Israel over it. This symbolized the transference of Israel's sins to the goat.[5] This innocent "scapegoat" would be led into the wilderness, taking away their sins. Years later, this symbolic ritual came to fulfillment in Jesus Christ. When John the Baptist saw Jesus coming, he cried out, "Behold, the Lamb of God, who takes away the sin of the world!"[6]

Typically, the Christian gospel that is preached from the pulpit only addresses the sins that *we've* committed. But what about those of us who have suffered under the weight of emotional or physical abuse? What about the years of negative feedback loops layered within the soil of our hearts? The good news is that Jesus takes all brokenness—that which we've shared and that which we've suffered—upon His shoulders and bears it to the wilderness. Allow His bearing your burden to free your heart and mind.

---

4   Ginger Lapid-Bogda Ph.D., *Bringing Out the Best in Everyone You Coach: Use the Enneagram System for Exceptional Results* (United States: McGraw-Hill Education, 2009).

5   Lev. 16:20-22

6   John 1:29b

> **→ Pray**
>
> Father, You are my greatest encourager. You are always trying to minister to me through the affirmation of others, but I have been so quick to discard it. Remove the defensive strategies I use to protect myself that also keep me from experiencing grace. Give me a discerning heart to hold fast to what is good and reject anything that is not from You.[7]

Day 19 Reflections:

How do you discard or deflect compliments and positive feedback? What can you do to internalize and hold onto encouragement longer?

How often do you catch yourself imagining being criticized by someone else? How do you internalize that criticism and make it your own to control the outcome?

Which of these internalized lies do you need to combat with truth today? (Sinner/ Forgiven; Abandoned/Adopted; Broken/Whole; Rejected/His; Failed/Victorious; Lost/Home; Not Special/Wonderfully Made; Worthless/Valued)

> **→ Respond**
>
> List the lies you are believing about yourself. Try to identify familial, cultural, or other sources behind the lies. Place your hand over the list and ask Jesus to fully and finally remove these lies within. Then rip up the piece of paper and throw it away.

7   1 Thes. 5:21

Day 20:

This Mystery

To them God chose to make known how great among the Gentiles are the riches

of the glory of this mystery, which is Christ in you, the hope of glory.

—Colossians 1:27

IN THE PHYSICAL WORLD, BOUNDARIES LIKE FENCES and signs are helpful because they define where our property ends and where someone else's begins. Similarly, God created boundaries for our souls. The journey of consciousness makes its first step when we begin to notice there is an *I* that is separate from our mothers or the rest of the world; that we, as Henry Cloud teaches, find where I end and someone else begins.[2]

Boundaries keep us from becoming doormats—people perpetually under others' control. While there are people who intrude upon our lives without permission,

God is where you are.

–Joan Chittister[1]

it's also true that the Individualist sometimes brings people into the recesses of their minds of their own volition. *Introjection* is the

---

1   Brett Webb-Mitchell, *Christly Gestures: Learning to be Members of the Body of Christ* (United Kingdom: W.B. Eerdmans, 2003), 240.

2   "What Are Healthy Boundaries?," Boundaries Books, accessed November 16, 2020, https://www.boundariesbooks.com/pages/what-are-healthy-boundaries.

"mechanism whereby we place inside our self-boundaries what properly belongs outside our boundaries," Jerome Wagner explains. Wagner gives the example of bringing a person inside our heads, turning them into a fantasized relationship and, when it inevitably fails, to meet those unnatural expectations, mourning the lost connection. Rather than grieving and letting the real or imaginary person go, the act of continual grieving keeps the other person always near, and yet never close.[3]

Another reason Four's might introject, or "swallow someone whole" as it's been said, is to fill the perceived emptiness inside. Sandra Maitri explains that Fours may "incorporate parts of those they love and admire. They take on and mimic their speech patterns and turns of phrase, their style of dress, ways of eating, thinking, and behaving; they adopt their forms of exercise—or lack thereof—and their attitudes and mannerisms."[4]

> Your gift of seeing what's missing was not given to make you feel more empty but to fill this world with God's life-giving presence.

But introjection is not only a negative trait: it can be a good thing if someone is said to be "just like her mother," because they've adopted her responsibility, empathy, or morality. The famous psychologist Sigmund Freud proposed that a child may introject and copy their father's behaviors and values to be *united* with him. In this way, the child is reconciled to his or her father and the lost connection is repaired.

Positive introjection shows that the journey toward consciousness does not end at separation, but with a reunification. The apostle Paul proclaimed that the mystery of the gospel is "Christ in you, the hope of glory."[5] In his letter to the Galatians he wrote, "It is no longer I who live, but Christ who lives in me."[6] Christains have

---

3 Wagner, *Nine Lenses*, 47.

4 Maitri, *The Spiritual Dimension*, 146.

5 Col. 1:27

6 Gal. 2:20

long believed that Christ takes up residence in our heart and soul, uniting us to Himself, the Spirit, and the Father.[7]

The Good News for Individualists is that by receiving Christ into our hearts, we are reconciled to our heavenly Father, from whose always-offered love we have separated ourselves. Not only is our relationship with Him restored, but we also undergo a character transformation being "conformed to the image of his Son."[8] As you take your eyes off of yourself and behold Christ, the Holy Spirit transforms you from an idealized self into His "image from one degree of glory to another."[9]

When Christ is introjected, rather than losing ourselves or becoming someone we're not, we become *more* of who we were created to be. We "put off" our old self—that melodramatic, moody, and that long-held feeling that we're bent or defective—and "put on" the new self that is creative, original, romantic, introspective, and emotionally attuned.[10] This new self, "Christ in us," allows us to internalize the message of wholeness and unity. When God says, "You are lovely," your heart replies with joy, "I am lovely." When you start absorbing what's missing in the world and view it as your own personal shortcoming, remember "Christ in you, the hope of glory."[11] Your gift of seeing what's missing was not given to make you feel more empty, but so that *you* can fill every crack and crevice in this world with God's life-giving presence—which right now is *in* you.

→ Pray

Father, oh how beautiful is this mystery of Christ in me, the hope of glory. You have made me beautiful, spotless, radiant, and blameless in Your eyes. Help me to believe it. Let Your life-giving presence well up within me like a spring and overflow onto those around me. Help me to focus my gaze on Jesus today as the Holy Spirit takes me to new degrees of glory.

---

7   John 17:20-26

8   Rom. 8:29

9   2 Cor. 3:18

10   Eph. 4:22-24

11   Col. 1:27

Day 20 Reflections:

How do you incorporate the qualities (good or bad) of someone you admire into your own psyche or outward presentation?

_____

_____

_____

_____

Who do you need to allow yourself to grieve and let go rather than continually mourning?

_____

_____

_____

_____

How does the mystical union of "Christ in you" challenge your perceived shortcomings and feelings of inferiority? How does it encourage you today?

_____

_____

_____

_____

→ Respond

Draw a face and use symbols and words to depict how you believe God sees His Son Jesus. Now, flip the paper over and draw how you believe God sees you. How are the two sides similar and different? Remind yourself that God now sees you in the same way He sees His Son because of "Christ in you."

Day 21:

Fantasyland

Look carefully then how you walk, not as unwise but as wise, making the

best use of the time, because the days are evil. Therefore do not be foolish, but

understand what the will of the Lord is.

—Ephesians 5:15-17

HAVE YOU EVER BEEN CAUGHT DAYDREAMING? I get caught so often that my son jokingly asks me, "Did you go to 'Ty-land' again?" In grade school, I daydreamed so much my teacher worried I had hearing problems. After a school-mandated trip to the ear doctor, my teacher was surprised to learn my hearing was quite excellent after all.

The world needs dreamers—those who can take the raw materials of creation and reorganize them into something revolutionary. In 1901, a young boy named Walter was born on the northwest side of Chicago. Walter grew up spending most days "in his own head," often putting his dreams into pictures. He took his first job as a commercial illustrator at the age of

> Being unique doesn't make you useful.
>
> –Ian Cron[1]

---

1 Cron and Stabile, *The Road Back to You Study Guide*, 40.

18 and went on to become perhaps the most famous animator, voice actor, and film producer ever. "Walt" Disney pioneered the American animation industry and won a record twenty-two Oscars. His imagination was the springboard for the most popular amusement park in the world and one of the most dominant businesses in history.[2]

Many Fours describe having a Disney-like imagination: "It's as if I'm watching multiple movies simultaneously, in full color and with accompanying soundtracks."[3] Or, as author Jessica Kantrowitz describes her interior world:

> Our fantasies only become fruitful when they are brought into everyday life.

> "When I was a child, I lived in my head. I read stories and wrote myself into those stories as an important character, helping to save the day. I was Fiver's confidante and Hazel's advisor in *Watership Down*. I walked with *Julie of the Wolves* through the frozen tundra ... I spent hours in those worlds, creating witty dialogue and orchestrating intense moments where I battled evil or gave up my powers to save a friend. I looked forward to nighttime when I could lie in bed for a half-hour or so before sleep, building on yesterday's scenes, escaping into one or another of my secret worlds."[4]

Fours have a rich interior life, but this gift must be stewarded. The average Individualist easily gets stuck in their own private fantasyland, which can become an inescapable house of mirrors where they fantasize about everything from falling in love to simply standing out among the crowd.

Though it's more pleasurable to spend time dreaming about writing that film or novel, the work required to develop the real skills to pull it off takes time, with feet planted in reality, and a dogged determination to follow through. Remember, our fantasies only become fruitful when they are brought into everyday life. Your legacy will not be determined by what you *dream* but by what you *do*. And there's only a limited amount of time to do it.

---

2 "Walt Disney." Biography.com, August 21, 2020, https://www.biography.com/business-fig- ure/walt-disney.

3 Lapid-Bogda, *Bringing Out the Best.*

4 Kantrowitz, *The Long Night*, 53-54.

Time is a resource we are forced to spend whether we want to or not; as you read this, you are "spending time" right now. This is why the apostle Paul admonished the Ephesian Christians to make the best use of their time, reminding the young congregation that the "days are evil." The clock is ticking: in sixty seconds, you'll be one minute closer to the end of your life. A fool forgets that they are "a mist that appears for a little time and then vanishes,"[5] but a wise person numbers their days.[6]

The Good News for Individualists is that dreamers aren't expected to change the world on their own—they have doers to come alongside. Although Walt Disney was perceived to be a Type A leader, those who knew him said he was shy, self-deprecating, and insecure about his abilities. Walt was able to accomplish so much largely because of an older, business-savvy brother, Roy, who helped turn Walt's dream into reality.[7] As a dreamer, you must look around to see who God has provided to turn your dreams into reality. Your potential for shaping the world will likely not be limited by your dreams but by whether or not you partner with others who can help bring those dreams to fruition here and now.

➜ Pray

Father, Your imagination is limitless. Every detail of every dream can be traced back to the God who creates. Thank You for fashioning my mind with Your imaginativeness and ingenuity, and for giving me vision to see what is not but what can be. I know that my time on earth is short; please give me the courage today to turn my dreams into reality and put them into action.

---

5   Jas. 4:14

6   Ps. 90:12

7   "Walt Disney." Biography.com, August 21, 2020, https://www.biography.com/business-fig-ure/walt-disney.

Day 21 Reflections:

What do you enjoy about being a dreamer? How has God used your imagination to add color and depth to the world?

_____

_____

_____

_____

What fantasies, daydreams, or running commentary has been going on in your head lately? What do these things reveal?

_____

_____

_____

_____

What dream have you been fantasizing about but procrastinating on?

_____

_____

_____

_____

➜ Respond

What skills do you fantasize about having? From this list, which ones could you begin developing now?

Day 22:

The Power of Symbols

For the word of the cross is folly to those who are perishing, but to us who are

being saved it is the power of God.

—1 Corinthians 1:18

I'M AN APPLE LOYALIST—MACBOOK, IPAD, APPLE WATCH, iPhone—you name it. Whether you are a fan or not, the iconic logo of an apple with a single bite out begs our respect. It has become a symbol of success and innovation throughout the world, taking its cue from powerful stories in both spiritual and scientific lore. Eve's insatiable desire for knowledge led her to bite into the forbidden fruit, and Sir Isaac Newton famously experienced his theory of gravity with the help of a falling apple. The Apple logo has therefore become an invitation for all to come and receive unlimited knowledge through its devices and join the ingenious tribe that is continuing to make history.

> Symbols are powerful because they are the visible signs of invisible realities.
>
> –St. Augustine

The purpose of a *symbol* is to transcend language, space, and time—to say more, to *mean more*, through representation than words alone could express. Graphic designer J.D. Reeves says symbols are the "perfect intersection of meaning and clarity."[1] The Individualist loves symbols and metaphors because they offer a medium to express the complexity they are always bearing within, to show their deepest truth when words seem to leave them misunderstood.

Through symbolism, Fours express a depth of meaning in the mundane that most people overlook—a walk through the woods, children playing on the beach, or an elderly couple holding hands. Their gift is to "say" more about the things that break the bounds of language. Regardless of the medium in which they express themselves, these creators illustrate the beautiful, painful, and profound ideas and feelings that the rest of us can't put into words. They are the "deep-sea divers of the psyche: they delve into the inner world of the human soul and return to the surface, reporting on what they have found."[2] When they talk, they speak poetically, lyrically, and intensely about the treasures they've found.

> Fours illustrate the beautiful, painful, and profound ideas and feelings that the rest of us can't put into words.

This act of symbolizing that which we cannot speak is known as *artistic sublimation*. It's taking socially unacceptable emotions and transforming them into actions or behavior that can be received by the rest of the world. For example, rather than lashing out at someone directly, you may turn your hostility into a poem, piece of art, drama, or indie album! I heard artist Billie Eilish say, "There are always going to be bad things. But you can write it down and make a song out of it."[3] That's why we love you. Your dramatizing of the things we feel everyday monumentalize our positive experiences and transform even our irritating grains of sand into pearls. Like a sponge, you absorb our feelings and become sad when we are sad, you get physically sick when we are emotionally ill, and then you render it all into a masterpiece for the world to admire.

The Book of Revelation is a wonder of artistic sublimation. The apostle John stretches language to the breaking point to inspire the fearful, persecuted

---

1   J.D. Reeves, "A History of Symbols," November 20, 2017, https://jdreeves.medium.com/a-history-of-symbols-a93626435bd2.

2   Riso and Hudson, *The Wisdom*, 200.

3   Flavia Medrut, "25 Billie Eilish Quotes to Embrace Your Most Authentic Self," Goalcast, October 7, 2020, https://www.goalcast.com/2020/10/07/billie-eilish-quotes/.

believers to faithfully endure and follow Christ's example of conquering through sacrifice. It traffics in well-known tropes to "reveal" the oppressive, antichrist power of all states that use the power of violence, religion, and money to cajole and entice people to fall in line. The strange symbolism of John's work is intended to encourage and prepare those who break from Caesar's worldview.

Our rich heritage in the faith is laden with transcendent symbols, which St. Augustine described as *visible* signs of *invisible* realities. The rainbow in Noah's story is a sign of God's covenant promise to us,[4] and the stairway in Jacob's dream is a spiritual bridge between earth and heaven.[5] The entire sacrificial system in the Old Testament is a visible sign for Christians of the forthcoming work of Christ.[6] Jesus commanded His disciples to practice baptism to represent one's initiation into the faith, imitating the death, burial, and resurrection into a new and different kind of life. He commanded them to receive the Lord's Supper as a way to regularly be reminded of the Divinity within the daily of incarnational life.[7] Imagine what our faith would look like without these things!

The Good News for Individualists can be found in the powerful symbol of the cross, which can't be reduced to words on a page or a philosophical thought in our heads. It evokes the strongest of emotions—resulting in a cry for salvation from the unbeliever and the loudest of praise from the believer. As an image bearer of the One who speaks in visions, dreams, words, and symbols—continue creating imagery that points the world to the invisible realities of God. Yes, we must make the gospel message clear with our words, but we must also be willing to use our creative talents to communicate those indescribable aspects of our faith when mere words aren't enough.

---

4   Gen. 9:13

5   Gen. 28:11-13

6   Heb. 10:19-20

7   Matt. 28:19; 26:26-29

→ Pray

Father, give me visions and dreams. I know that English is not Your primary language. Unleash my full creative potential to bring greater depth to a church living in shallow times. Thank You for giving me such rich symbols in the Scriptures to feast on for spiritual nourishment—namely the cross of Christ, which gives me Divine power to believe and change.

Day 22 Reflections:

What does the symbol of the cross mean to you?

Have you ever thought of the command in Genesis 1:28 as a call to create and cultivate symbols as part of your spiritual work and witness? Why or why not?

What do you think this spiritual work looks like practically in the church?

→ Respond

Have a conversation with a pastor or leader about equipping those in your church to use the arts more in their own personal calling or spiritual service.

Day 23:

Wrestling with God

I cry aloud to God, aloud to God, and he will hear me. In the day of my trouble

I seek the LORD; in the night my hand is stretched out without wearying; my

soul refuses to be comforted. When I remember God, I moan; when I meditate,

my spirit faints. You hold my eyelids open; I am so troubled that I cannot speak.

—Psalm 77:1-4

ONE OF THE FOUNDATIONAL TALES OF THE Hebrew people is Jacob's wrestling match with God at the Jabbok River. The trickster has spent most of his life running from problems and staying one step ahead of the consequences. In fact, he's on one side of the Jabbok because his brother Esau (and his army) was on the other! As darkness falls, an "Unknown Traveler" wrestles with Jacob as he lies near the water's edge, and there they struggle until the horizon begins to brighten.

> Wrestling with God is a sign of intimacy. You can't wrestle with someone you're far away from.
>
> –Jon Acuff

Suddenly, this Unknown Traveler who we discover in the story is actually God, "touched" Jacob's hip socket and his hip was wrenched out of joint. In a surprising twist, Jacob (the runner, the "soft" one who fled from fights) has finally been backed into a corner and found the courage to engage. God says, "Let me go," but Jacob replies, "I will not let you go until you bless me." The change of character has been fulfilled and Jacob is now ready to take the mantle of Patriarch: "Your name shall no longer be called Jacob, but Israel, for you have striven with God and with men, and have prevailed."[1]

From this story, it appears that God delights in people who aren't afraid to strive and struggle. The "People of God" received this name to share their foundational posture toward the Divine, and Israel means "one who struggles with God." Though such an assertive stance may feel counterintuitive to some, it comes naturally to the Individualist. Does your journal reveal a collection of "wrestling" prayers? Are you more confident than most that you will not be reprimanded for your doubts or questions but rewarded? Brutal honesty with God and others is not just ideal; it is the only way to maintain a healthy soul.

> God delights in people who aren't afraid to strive and struggle.

Facing life's harsh realities isn't easy, but it is necessary to move forward and grow. (I've already confessed that the emotive Book of Psalms was my least favorite book of the Bible for years. It has taken a lot of time and effort to replace my "well-worded requests" with raw emotion, and I'm often still tempted to fear God's punishment if I say what I really feel.) As I approach my fourth decade of life, I've learned that what has worked for me in the past isn't working anymore. As the novelist and activist James Baldwin said, "All artists, if they are to survive, are forced, at last, to tell the whole story, to vomit the anguish up."[2]

As a Four, one of the reasons you might liberally share the authentic truth of your struggles is because you are constantly trying to discover who you are. You are not afraid to go down the dark rabbit hole to better understand your complex emotional experiences and history.[3] This posture of self-revelation is a gift to

---

1   Gen. 32:28

2   Riso and Hudson, *The Wisdom*, 177.

3   Ibid, 179.

the community because it means you won't be shocked or paralyzed by others' confessions, but rather accepting, supportive, and compassionate to their stories.

Your desire to draw emotional truths into the light will lead to healthier environments at home and elsewhere as you challenge those around you to face what's in the shadows.[4] A healthy Four who has done their hard heart work will have a quiet strength about them that draws others into their safe presence.

The Good News for Individualists is that God loves those who strive and struggle. But remember, Jacob's struggle left him with more than a new name; he also left the Jabbok with a limp—a lifelong reminder of the struggle. Not only that, he also stepped into the dawn with a new way of seeing the world. After the dust settled, the wonder of what just occurred overcame the newly-minted patriarch, and he renamed the place Peniel, saying, "For I have seen God face to face, and yet my life is preserved."[5] That same day, upon reconciling with the brother he so long feared, he exclaimed, "for truly to see your face is like seeing the face of God."[6]

Your willingness to wrestle and share the tale can encourage others to engage deeply with life's darkness so that they may also come out on the other side with a new name, scars to share with others, and a new way of seeing those in whom the Divine image resides.

→ Pray

Father, I admit that I sometimes hesitate to bring my burdens to others. I've been ignored and rejected too many times. Thank You for giving me the courage to pour out my heart to You with brutal honesty. I know You can take it. I commit myself to strive for Your blessing everyday. Give me the courage to set an example of vulnerability for those around me today.

---

4   Kacie Berghoef and Melanie Bell, *The Modern Enneagram: Discover Who You Are and Who You Can Be* (United States: Callisto Media Incorporated, 2017), 135.

5   Gen. 32:30 NRSV

6   Gen. 33:10 NRSV

Day 23 Reflections:

Was "wrestling with God" encouraged or discouraged in your church growing up? What about now?

_____

_____

_____

_____

When have you sought to draw emotional truths out into the light? Did it go well or poorly?

_____

_____

_____

_____

What practical steps can you take to set an example and build an atmosphere of authenticity?

_____

_____

_____

_____

➜ Respond

Lead a devotional on Psalm 77 with your roommates, family, or small group.

Day 24:

Blind Spots in Love

Love is patient and kind; love does not envy or boast; it is not arrogant or rude.

It does not insist on its own way; it is not irritable or resentful; it does not

rejoice at wrongdoing, but rejoices with the truth. Love bears all things, believes

all things, hopes all things, endures all things.

—1 Corinthians 13:4-7

MOST FOURS CAN'T STAND THE IDEA OF perfectly calm and predictable relationships. Even the most mature of us occasionally give into the desire to spice up normal misunderstandings and annoyances with an extra layer of drama. This behavior is especially true of younger and unhealthy Individualists. Drama makes a good story—which is entered into and then set aside—but a terrible way of life. Richard Rohr insightfully points out, "The idea of Romeo and Juliet getting married, having children, and leading a wholly 'normal'

> If we wait for some people to become agreeable or attractive before we begin to love them, we will never begin.
>
> –Thomas Merton[1]

---

1   Thomas Merton, *No Man Is an Island* (United States: Shambhala, 2005), 179.

married life would be too banal; it would impair the universality and greatness of their love."[2] The greatest love story of all time *is* what it *is* because it's fraught with tension (and more than a tinge of youthful infatuation and melodrama).

While you may enjoy—or at least feel the need for—the exciting twists and turns found in *Romeo and Juliet*, the rest of the world has a harder time accepting this in reality. The Individualist says, "What is true love without desperate sonnets over unrequited love, intense balcony soliloquies, heart-wrenching break-ups, and climactic reunions?"

The apostle Paul lays out a deeply poetic roadmap for the way of love in Chapter 13 of his pastoral letter to the Corinthians. When we just skim this chapter for positive inspiration at weddings, we miss the true gravity of Paul's words, which have much less to say about romantic love and marriage than they do about being a new kind of human. As a way to turn this gem, let's look at what love is *not* to help shine a light on some of the blind spots Fours say they've encountered. We've already discussed envy in the "Spears of Envy" devotion, so let's look at some of the other words Paul uses here. Not all of these may apply to you right now, but might be helpful things to watch out for under stress.

> God bears with us in love even when we fail at love.

First, love is not *arrogant*. Arrogance is, at its core, an overestimation of our own importance. While believing yourself to be God's gift to the world is an obvious kind, a more subtle strain is to overly fixate on your own suffering, to the ignorance and lessening of others' or becoming so absorbed with our own immediate emotional concerns that we become uninterested in the feelings or problems of others. Riso and Hudson explain that "Fours under stress begin to exaggerate their importance in others' lives. They remind others of the many benefits that they have derived from their association with the Four, take credit for others' happiness, and find little ways to increase people's dependency on them."[3]

Second, love is not *rude*. Rudeness can look like withdrawing from people and social events—standing off to the side with a haughty posture. Being introverted

---

2   Rohr and Ebert, *The Enneagram*, 104.

3   Riso and Hudson, *The Wisdom*, 198.

or reserved is not a character flaw, but refusing to engage due to feelings of superiority is destructive to the self and others. Then, if a Four *does* engage but feels misunderstood by a lover, boss, or teammate, they may abruptly lash out, sending shrapnel in all directions to anyone in the near vicinity.

Third, love is not *irritable*. When unsatisfied, Fours feel shortchanged by life and become abnormally insensitive, parading their hurt feelings and moping around. While sulking, they may avoid their own responsibilities and make others feel guilty for their undeserved plight. Suzanne Stabile notes, "It's hard to learn to be with someone who so desperately wants to be satisfied, and at the same time cannot seem to find satisfaction with what is."[4]

Fourth, love is not *resentful*. When a Four spends a lifetime seeking the fulfillment of their desire and finds that nothing on this earth can satisfy them, they may begin to believe someone is withholding that fulfillment. They may project the frustration (which is often unprocessed shame) onto others, leaving them to feel they are not enough or worthy of the Individualists' attention or with the demoralizing impression that the Four loves them "even though it makes me unhappy."[5]

The Good News for Individualists is that God bears with us in love even when we fail at love. The Father sent His Son, Jesus, to show us the way of love and gently point out our blind spots. As with *Romeo and Juliet*, Jesus' life also ends dramatically, as He chooses death because He can't bear the thought of being separated from us forever. Yet this was no flight of adolescent fancy, but a conscious choice to receive the worst humanity can heap upon a person and return absolute love. Such an example of life-giving love reverberates more strongly than all the Bard's works combined. Through the prism of Christ, the full spectrum of divine compassion has been made visible to us. If you have seen and tasted this radiant love, go and love others in the same way today.

---

4   Stabile, *The Path Between Us*, 115.

5   Palmer, *The Enneagram in Love and Work*, 121.

> ### → Pray
>
> Father, You are love itself. When it comes to being selfless, my love sometimes falls incredibly short. Help me to bear with others as You bear with me. Enable me by Your Holy Spirit to demonstrate kindness and patience from the well of Your steadfast love, which endures forever.

Day 24 Reflections:

How has God shown you patience, kindness, and steadfast love through all your ups and downs?

_____

_____

_____

_____

Who do you need to show more kindness and patience toward?

_____

_____

_____

Which aspect of Paul's definition of love do you struggle with the most? What can you do about it?

_____

_____

_____

_____

> ### → Respond
>
> Identify a person or group that you don't feel like engaging with right now as a result of unmet needs. List the unwritten expectations you have for them. Are they realistic? Try reevaluating any unrealistic expectations and re-engage with more patience.

Day 25:

Surviving the Real World

He was in the world, and the world was made through him, yet the world did

not know him. He came to his own, and his own people did not receive him.

—John 1:10-11

WHEN JESUS SHOWED UP ON THE SCENE, He played the prophet's role of an outsider. His parabolic language and upside-down values made people look at Him with questioning eyes. Have you ever felt this way—as though everything within you said *I belong somewhere else*? The traditional Western workplace is not as welcoming of Individualists compared to other personality types. Fours value meaning over money, excellence over efficiency, quality over productivity, and the underdog over the CEO. That's why it can seem like you need a survival guide to make it in the real world!

> I shouldn't be expected
> to do what mere
> mortals have to do.
>
> –Riva[1]

The Four's superpower is inspiring others to cultivate the same passion for depth and meaning as they naturally experience. They make great actors, artists, writers, editors, designers, teachers, researchers,

---

1   Riso and Hudson, *The Wisdom*, 189.

entrepreneurs, counselors, and activists. If unable to find a suitable harmonization between what they feel to be their calling and the pragmatic needs of their daily employment, they may very quickly disintegrate into depression and question the purpose of work (or, in deeply unhealthy states, even life). The point being, Fours sense a deep need to find their daily tasks meaningful. In the workplace, Fours want a job with an eccentric edge and a unique approach, where they feel respected for their ideas and can avoid the mundane work of "ordinary" people.[2]

But reality is primarily made of the mundane, and so the main challenge for the Individualists is to *make* and *discover* meaning in their daily lives and work. Fours feel stressed when they don't feel understood or are easily dismissed—often providing deep insights on why people aren't getting along. They may raise red flags on what's missing and offer suggestions to

> Don't buy into the lie that your struggle in the real world is a sign that something is wrong with you.

make the workplace more whole, aesthetic, functional, or balanced but these uncommon suggestions may not be received well.[3]

How can you survive when your wiring and workplace collide? You must first learn to appreciate your genuine talents and not envy the more "glamorous" gifts of others. Do not fear being upstaged by your coworkers or even view yourself as in direct competition with them. Rather, seek to encourage and inspire, being content to fill the world with beauty, even if others ultimately receive the credit. Imitate Jesus, who took the path of radical descent, of downward mobility, "[emptying] himself, by taking the form of a servant."[4]

The Good News for Individualists is Jesus knows what it feels like not to be well-received—to be misunderstood and outside of His time. He was often the recipient of awkward, dismissive glances because people didn't know what box to put Him in. When you struggle to be understood, valued, or taken seriously, don't despair or give into the temptation to belittle yourself. Don't buy into the lie that your struggle in the real world is a sign that something is wrong with you: it's

---

2   Palmer, *The Enneagram in Love and Work*, 122-124.

3   Chestnut, *The 9 Types of Leadership*, 139-140.

4   Phil. 2:7

not. You were not meant for a different place or time, but for the here and now, to bring life into the world in ways that only you can.

→ Pray

Father, You are *El Roi*, the God who sees me. I often feel abandoned or unsupported, but You are always there looking upon me with love. It's often a struggle to fit in. Help me to embrace my uniqueness and remember my inherent worth. Give me the Spirit's power to show mercy to those who haven't received or welcomed me—following in the example of Jesus.

Day 25 Reflections:

Which personal value of yours seems to conflict the most with the western workplace?

_____

_____

_____

_____

Where do you struggle in your work relationships? What can you do on your end to improve the relationship?

_____

_____

_____

_____

What is the most challenging piece of advice you want to work on from today's reading?

_____

_____

_____

_____

➜ Respond

Solicit positive feedback by asking a boss or co-worker what you bring to the team that is unique and valuable.

Day 26:

The Dark Night

Then Jesus was led up by the Spirit into the wilderness to be tempted

by the devil.

—Matthew 4:1

EMILY CAME TO ME AND BRAVELY ADMITTED that she was struggling with depression. For weeks, she was so depressed she could not even muster the energy to get out of bed in the morning. As a new spiritual leader, I was inexperienced in dealing with matters of depression, and I have to admit, I was shamefully unhelpful. I didn't know what to say or how to refer her to a mental health professional; I didn't even know where (or if) to point her to in the Bible, so I googled "depression" and found Psalm 42. To my surprise, reading the Psalm did not cure her depression! In my youthful lack of empathy, I grew irritated and suspected that her inability to climb out of her dark emotions meant that she was steeped in unbelief. Poor girl—I still regret the indelicate way I held her and others with similar struggles in those days.

> In the dark night of the soul, bright flows the river of God.
>
> –St. John of the Cross[1]

---

1 St. John of the Cross, *Dark Night of the Soul* (N.p.: Whitaker House, 2017).

Have you found yourself in a "dark night of the soul" and been told or believed it was because your faith wasn't strong enough, as though the darkness were a figment of your imagination or due to some shortcoming within yourself? Seasons of depression are common to all people—from the least spiritually-aware to the strongest of saints, and yet is viewed by many in the church as a "disease" only afflicting the weak. Many churches are unfortunately lagging behind the culture in dealing with matters of mental health.

When the waves of negative emotions come crashing, it might feel physically impossible to swim against the current. As self-doubt creeps in, you may start to wonder if you'll ever feel unbroken or content, if the deep waters will swallow you whole. Inconsolable, you may begin sinking—withdrawing more and more from others into the deep abyss.

> The clouds will not cover the landscape of your heart forever; eventually, the sun will break through.

Individualists deal with depression differently from each other and from other personality types. For some, the sadness is an obvious, constant companion, while for others, it is buried beneath an upbeat, buoyant facade. Either way, one of the first steps to take is to seek help—it's not a sign of failure to admit you cannot tread water forever. Aside from taking care of your mental health by seeking the help of a qualified professional, be sure to take care of your physical self—invest in hobbies and life-giving activities and exercise. Finally, be sure to confide in trusted companions. Seek the company of those who love and support you and take an interest in their lives as well. A Four who can shift attention from self toward the needs of others can more easily break free from the spiralling cul-de-sac of depression.[2]

As you emerge from your dark night of the soul, you may find that you have a more profound acceptance and understanding of yourself. As one Four shared, "Experiencing my pain leads to feeling more connected with myself, which then alleviates the pain of feeling disconnected and misunderstood. Thus when a dark feeling hits, my impulse is to hang out with it and get to the bottom of it."[3]

---

2   Palmer, *The Enneagram in Love and Work*, 118.

3   Chestnut, *The Complete Enneagram*, 291.

You may also emerge from the dark night having a more profound understanding of human nature. As Riso and Hudson note about Fours, "they can see the devil and the angel."[4] That's a fitting statement considering the fact that Jesus literally saw the devil during His dark night of the soul. At the very outset of His ministry, the Spirit of God sent Him into the wilderness. For forty days, He experienced hunger, thirst, a threatening environment, and temptation—through *no fault* of His own but to prepare Him for the work ahead.

Finally, understand that seasons of depression—like life—come in waves. The clouds will not cover the landscape of your heart forever; eventually, the sun will break through and you will experience relief. But as with the clouds, so with the sun: the bright days will come and go as well. As we grow, we can better prepare to handle each wave as it comes.

The Good News for Individualists is that when a healthy Four comes out of a dark night of the soul, it is like a butterfly emerging from its cocoon. As Dr. Elisabeth Kubler-Ross says, "The most beautiful people we have known are those who have known defeat, known suffering, known struggle, known loss, and have found their way out of the depths. ... Beautiful people do not just happen."[5] Our Savior—who "learned obedience through what he suffered"[6]—holds in love those who are not able to see the light at the end of the tunnel.

If you are in a dark place today, find hope in these words from Barbara Brown Taylor:

> "... when, despite all my best efforts, the lights have gone off in my life (literally or figuratively, take your pick), plunging me into the kind of darkness that turns my knees to water, nonetheless I have not died. The monsters have not dragged me out of bed and taken me back to their lair. The witches have not turned me into a bat. Instead, I have learned things in the dark that I could never have learned in the light, things that have saved my life over and over again, so that there is really only one logical conclusion. I need darkness as much as I need light."[7]

---

4   Riso and Hudson, *Personality Types,* 149.

5   Loughrige and Calhoun, *Spiritual Rhythms*, 109.

6   Heb. 5:8

7   Barbara Brown Taylor, "Barbara Brown Taylor: In Praise of Darkness," Time, April 17, 2014, https://tinyurl.com/yywg3mde.

→ Pray

Father, even when I walk through the valley of death, I know You are with me to comfort, protect, and reassure.[8] Thank You for sending Jesus who battled through the most painful night, sweating and spilling blood, but re-emerged from the tomb of death to bring the light of hope into my life. Because of Him, I know that "weeping may tarry for the night, but joy comes in the morning."[9]

Day 26 Reflections:

What does the dark night of the soul feel like? How long does it last?

_____

_____

_____

How have you been mistreated by others in seasons of depression? What is one thing you wish Christians knew about seasons of depression?

_____

_____

_____

What will be your go-to activity the next time you start experiencing depression symptoms?

_____

_____

_____

→ Respond

If you are having difficulty regulating your emotions, aren't performing at work/school, aren't enjoying the same activities you used to, are experiencing disruptions in sleep or eating habits, or are grieving trauma or a relationship, contact a mental health professional or pastor to take a step toward healing.

8 Ps. 23:4

9 Ps. 30:5

Day 27:

Job's Friends

Eliphaz speaking to his suffering friend Job] Is not your evil abundant? There is no end to your iniquities.

—Job 22:5

AFTER EMILY, THE YOUNG WOMAN STRUGGLING WITH depression I tried to "fix" moved on, I found myself in a similar season of depression myself a few years later. I already shared with you the grueling reality of infertility we experienced, but what made it worse were the insensitive people. Perhaps you've experienced something similar: I was mentoring a young man during this difficult period, who, to my surprise asked, "Do you think God won't let Lindsey get pregnant because of past sin in your lives?" I was so stunned by such a horribly misguided question that I didn't know what to say. To this day, his words stay with us.

> It is better to drink of deep griefs than to taste shallow pleasures.
>
> –William Hazlitt[1]

If you have experienced trauma while living in Christian community, you've likely experienced something

---

1   William Hazlitt and William Ernest Henley, *The Collected Works of William Hazlitt: Memoirs of Thomas Holcroft* (United Kingdom: J. M. Dent & Company, 1902), 413.

similar. A few of our friends wondered if our suffering was a result of not trying hard enough: "It's probably anxiety. If you just try harder not to worry, I'm sure you'll get pregnant." Or, "Have you prayed more about this? Are you reading your Bible every day? Are you getting enough sleep and eating healthy?"

It's not that the Body of Christ is less caring than others—rather, I would suggest our understanding of God's economy needs to be updated. In many ways, Christians not only think of God in pre-New Testament terms, we also think in pre-*Old* Testament terms.

The story of Job in the Hebrew Scriptures immortalizes some of the worst responses to grief in all of literature. Set in the age before Abraham heeded God's call, the understandings of divine justice were straightforward: the gods were only as faithful to you as you were to them. If you faithfully offer sacrifices, they will

> Show us that what we need most are not answers but God's presence.

offer their blessing; if not, well, watch out for marauding raiders, fire from heaven, and house-destroying winds.[2] No covenant of eternal protection, no overtures of divine love, just straightforward, quid pro quo transactions.

But as his story progresses, we see that Job's God is different—even if he and his clueless friends don't yet realize it. While Job spent chapters protesting his innocence (and therefore, under the pre-covenantal understanding of divine justice, undeserving of his sufferings), his friends assume he's deluded or lying— especially given the level of tragedy. Our God—*Job's God*—doesn't work like that. Blessings and tragedies are not meted out as divine rewards and punishments, but rather, they are part of an eternal, ineffable plan set in motion by the Maker of the cosmos. God does not directly answer Job's demands, but he does flatly denounce Job's friends' accusations against God's servant, based on an entirely wrongheaded view of the Divine.

Such a long view of God's workings ought to compel the faithful. Rather than look for "causes" of pain and tragedy, they simply show up and offer their presence to a hurting world—and in particular, those we have the honor to sit together

---

2   Job 1:13-19

with in mourning, bearing witness to pain through presence. Fours are innately gifted with the ability to mourn with those who mourn and desperately long for companions who can offer the same gift when suffering knocks at their own door.

The Good News for Individualists is that all of us can get better at bearing one another's burdens. Life, though brimming over with joy, is also full of disappointment and tragedy, offering many opportunities to gain proficiency in presence. Though I am saddened by my lack of understanding for that young woman's sufferings years ago, I have learned better how to sit with those in pain; I hope the young man who so jarringly answered my own family's pain has also grown in this area. Teach the world—starting with those nearest you—how to be the sort of caring community you want around when pain shows itself in your own life. Show us that what we need most are not *answers* but God's *presence,* which is most evident in this world when God's people show up.

→ Pray

Father, thank You for defending me against the heartless, controlling comforters that surround me with their false piety and pithy statements. I praise You for sending Jesus, who is able to sympathize with me. When I am weak and in pain and begin to demand answers of You like Job, remind me that You are God and I am not. Grant me the Spirit's power to suffer and grieve with humility—and the drive to help create a community of people adept at rejoicing and mourning.

Day 27 Reflections:

When have you experienced sympathy without feeling like the person was trying to fix you?

_____

_____

_____

_____

What is the most insensitive thing someone has said to you when you were grieving?

_____

_____

_____

_____

How can you help people grieve or understand a more holistic view of grief in your church?

_____

_____

_____

_____

→ Respond

Prepare a lesson on grief or start a grief group.

Day 28:

Living Between the Mountains

On the next day, when they had come down from the mountain, a great

crowd met him.

—Luke 9:37

HAVE YOU EVER HAD ONE OF THOSE mountaintop experiences? As a new Chrisitan, I packed up the car and set off for many exhilarating retreats, national conferences, spring break service projects, and summer mission trips. It's easy to love God and others on the mountain, when God seems as close as the sky He made, but these experiences are short-lived. Though we want to stay in these special moments where heaven and earth collide, at some point, we have to come back down and re-enter reality.

> We don't become more spiritual by becoming less human.
>
> —Eugene Peterson[1]

In the Gospels, the transfiguration occurs when Jesus takes Peter, John, and James up on a mountaintop to pray. Praying with Jesus was a regular thing for all the disciples, but this time it's different. As Jesus prayed, His face became radiant, His clothes dazzling

---

1 Eugene Peterson, *Tell It Slant: A Conversation on the Language of Jesus in His Stories and Prayers* (United States: Eerdmans Publishing Company, 2012), 45.

white, and two of the most famous prophets in their people's history—Moses and Elijah—appeared out of nowhere, talking with their teacher. Peter, John, and James woke from a heavy sleep just in time to see Jesus' glory and the Father's voice coming out of the clouds, reminding them to be quiet and pay attention.[2] Not a bad prayer meeting.

What is most striking to me is the next verse in this narrative: "On the next day, when they had come down from the mountain, a great crowd met him."[3] After this mountaintop experience, I'm sure Peter, James, and John were still riding high and trying to make sense of it all. Perhaps they felt a bit superior for being privy to such an experience that no other ordinary person had witnessed, but once they get back down, they are met by a large group of men and women—with needs. Oh yes, back to real life.

Jesus got His hands dirty.

To be clear, Jesus came so that you may "have life and have it abundantly."[4] God gave your body dopamine and serotonin to provide adrenaline rushes and heighten your pleasure, and the same is true for your soul. God created you to have exhilarating experiences. However, the majority of life is lived between the mountains—an often disappointing journey filled with work that often feels way too mundane.

Timothy Keller, in his book *Every Good Endeavor*, explained that work for the ancient Greeks was considered a curse. Aristotle said that the qualification for a worthwhile life was one in which you didn't have to labor. In his society, slaves and craftsmen did all the manual labor—working for others was seen as a way of enslaving yourself—so that the elite could be freed up to engage in the arts.[5] While the idea of delegating all forms of manual labor to others might sound appealing, we must re-examine that thought in light of who God is. Anglican minister Phillip Jensen put it this way: "If God came into the world, what would he be like? For the ancient Greeks, he might have been a philosopher-king. The

---

2 Luke 9:28-36

3 Luke 9:37

4 John 10:10

5 Timothy Keller, *Every Good Endeavor: Connecting Your Work to God's Work* (United States: Penguin Publishing Group, 2012), 45.

ancient Romans might have looked for a just and noble statesman. But how does the God of the Hebrews come into the world? As a carpenter."[6]

The Good News for Individualists is that Jesus got His hands dirty; whether working as a craftsman or an itinerant teacher, He found fulfillment in work. As a carpenter, He built tables and chairs, and as a teacher, He fed the hungry, healed the sick, and washed His disciples' feet. Jesus demonstrated that *all* work has value, especially when we can find the sort of labor that harmonizes our daily activities with our broader calling. Let this be motivation for you the next time you want to quit because what you are doing seems to lack any meaning—all labor, if done to bring life into the world Christ stepped into, has meaning.

➜ Pray

Father, You are the Life Giver. In Your presence there is abundant joy. I'm thankful for all of the transcendent encounters I've had with You. Help me to embrace life between the mountains. Enable me to see the beauty in all of the ordinary things I do today. Just as Jesus washed my feet, help me to find meaning today in getting my hands dirty serving others.

---

6   Ibid, 49.

Day 28 Reflections:

What is one of your greatest mountaintop experiences? Why was it so memorable?

_____

_____

_____

_____

What are you doing right now that is meaningful? What tasks at home or responsibilities at work do you find yourself avoiding?

_____

_____

_____

_____

In light of who God is, how might you need to redefine your definition of meaningful?

_____

_____

_____

_____

➜ Respond

Practice the "hardest-first" technique. Create a to-do list for today, and then reorder the list putting the "hardest" tasks first. Spending your energy on resolving these things quicker will eliminate the prolonged anxiety caused by avoiding.[7]

---

7 Moser, *The Enneagram of Discernment*, 148.

Day 29:

Letting Go of the Past

So Joseph said to his brothers, "Come near to me, please." And they came

near. And he said, "I am your brother, Joseph, whom you sold into Egypt. ...

And he kissed all his brothers and wept upon them. After that his brothers

talked with him.

—Genesis 45:4,15

WHEN I WAS IN MIDDLE SCHOOL, MY parents were invited into a home Bible study and immediately got hooked. The caring people gathering to share their lives together and spend time contemplating Scripture were experiences unknown to our family. Soon after, they began taking us to a small church in a neighboring community. But the residents of our small town were less than enthusiastic about my parents' new denomination: my mother was fired from her teaching job because the private school feared she might proselytize her students, and we received a letter in the mail from an anonymous person who ended with the words, "You cannot hide."

> When the past calls,
>
> let it go to voicemail.
>
> –Ian Cron[1]

---

1   Cron and Stabile, *The Road Back to You,* 166.

Following Jesus' call, as we understood it, was the best decision we ever made, but it was not without consequences. Beginning with that experience and reverberating throughout my life, I've learned that attempting to protect yourself from getting hurt in this world is futile. Animosity, ill will, hatred, and perpetual opposition has existed since the beginning.[2] The question we should ask is not, "Will I get hurt?" but rather "How can I pursue healing and wholeness?"

When Joseph was a young boy, he journeyed to the land of Canaan with his parents—Jacob and Rachel—and many siblings. Since he was the youngest son and born from his father's favorite wife, Joseph's eleven older brothers began to suspect that he was Jacob's favorite.[3] When Joseph

> God is able to heal the deep scars caused by relational trauma.

was presented with an expensive, ornate coat that made him stand out even more, their suspicions were confirmed, and they began to quietly fume with jealousy. Their father's favoritism was bad enough, but the nail in the coffin came when Joseph repeated two dreams in which his parents and brothers were bowing down to him. One may wonder why Joseph was so forthcoming with these dreams, knowing they would severely provoke his brothers.

One day, Joseph visits his brothers in the fields near Shechem. Seizing an opportunity, the brothers throw "this dreamer" into a pit rather than killing him outright—thanks to Reuben, who plans to return and save him. A short while later, the rest of the brothers spot a caravan passing by and decide to sell him as a slave, thereby making some money off of his demise *and* sending him into the far-flung obscurity of Egyptian slavery. To make a long story short, through divine providence—and many trials—Joseph ends up as Pharaoh's viceroy. Yet, though he is now second-in-command over all Egypt, has a wife and children, and seems to have found all that was taken from him, he is still carrying the emotional wounds—the trauma—of his previous life.

Can you imagine the whirlwind of emotions Joseph feels when a famine brings his brothers to Egypt to beg for bread a few decades later? If your own betrayers and would-be murders came before you and the power was now in your hands,

---

2 Gen. 3:15

3 Gen. 37–44

what would you do with the men who stole your freedom and the love of your father and mother? As the brothers bow before him, not knowing to whom they plead for help, Joseph remembers the dreams God gave him as a child, and decides to conceal his identity at first. Eventually, though, he loses all control and reveals himself. He falls into his brothers' arms, kissing and weeping upon them.[4]

Are you still carrying around a suitcase of past hurts? All people struggle on some level to forgive, but Riso and Hudson warn that Individualists have a tendency "to nurse wounds and hold on to negative feelings about those who have hurt them."[5] An unhealthy Four may continually dwell on the past to give their present pain a purpose, reinforce a victim mentality, or blame those people who put their lives on an unfair trajectory.

The Good News for Individualists is that God is able to heal the deep scars caused by relational trauma, both small and great. Just as the prophet Isaiah predicted, the Messiah came and was "crushed for our iniquities"—those we have done and have been done to us—so that by "his wounds we are healed."[6] Jesus has provided a healing balm for the wounds that continue to tear open and swell within. The first step is to *let go* of our accusers, abusers, betrayers, or neglectors that are weighing us down. But it's important to recognize that forgiveness does not mean forgetting the injustice or giving them a pass; it does not mean pretending the wound was never opened. Rather, it is releasing the person to "him who judges justly"[7] so that *you* can be free of the prison your hurt has put you in. From what hurts, injustices, and traumas do you need to be released? Whatever they are, *that* is why Jesus came.[8]

---

4   Gen. 45:15

5   Riso and Hudson, *The Wisdom*, 180.

6   Isa. 53:5

7   1 Pet. 2:23

8   Luke 4:18

→ Pray

Father, You are scandalously merciful. Oh, the depths of Your kindness toward Your enemies! Give me the same tears that Jesus had when He wept over Jerusalem, and the same forgiving words He uttered to His executioners at the cross. Help me to never forget the ways I've hurt You so that I might have strength to forgive those who've injured me.

Day 29 Reflections:

What hostility, neglect, or opposition from others are you still carrying with you?

_____

_____

_____

What is preventing you from letting go of past hurt or a lost relationship? What do you fear will happen if you do?

_____

_____

_____

What soul work do you think had to happen in Joseph's heart for him to weep over his brothers? Have you asked God to give you tears for your enemies?

_____

_____

_____

→ Respond

Write a "Goodbye Letter" to help you let go of someone from your past who has either helped you or hurt you. List any special or painful memories with that person, the lessons you've learned from the relationship, and something you want them to know.

Day 30:

Redeeming Our Suffering

As for you, you meant evil against me, but God meant it for good, to bring it

about that many people should be kept alive, as they are today.

—Genesis 50:20

PERPETUA WAS A YOUNG, WELL-EDUCATED, AFRICAN NOBLEWOMAN living in Carthage near the end of the second century. At the tender age of 22, as a new mother holding her infant in her arms, she stood before her pagan father, who pleaded that she recant her faith, fearing that Emperor Septimius Severus would take her life. But, as her legend shares, Perpetua boldly stood her ground, saying, "Do you see this vessel—waterpot or whatever it may be? Can it be called by any other name than what it is?" "No," he replied. "So also I cannot call myself by any other name than what I am—a Christian."

> We're coming to realize that a relationship with Christ is not intended to cover up the dark side of life, but rather to illuminate a path through it.
>
> –Dan B. Allender[1]

---

1 Dan B. Allender and Tremper Longman, *Bold Love* (United States: NavPress, 1992), 11.

Perpetua and another young mother, Felicity were indeed eventually dragged to the amphitheater by the Emperor's agents to be publicly beheaded for their beliefs.[2] Perpetua, Felicity, and the voices of all the faithful martyrs across space and time are heard by God, their deaths watering the ground from which the church has offered peace to the world for thousands of years—as the church father Tertullian professed, "the blood of the martyrs is the seed of the church."[3]

Their suffering and ours, from the smallest moments of frustration with this imperfect world to the most traumatic encounters with evil, bear the fruit of purpose out of the soil of pain. We see this in Joseph's story that we looked at yesterday: little did Joseph know that

> Allow your past suffering to show you where you ought to go next.

the pit of death that his jealous brothers threw him into would be the beginning of an unforeseen plan to rescue his people from an unprecedented famine. The betrayal of his brothers and accompanying trauma is thankfully *not* the end of his story because God gave Joseph's pain a purpose. He flipped the script and turned his suffering into a plan of salvation.

The apostle Paul peculiarly writes, "Now I rejoice in my sufferings for your sake, and in my flesh I am filling up what is lacking in Christ's afflictions for the sake of his body, that is, the church."[4] What does Paul think is lacking? Are Christ's sufferings not sufficient for us? No, Paul is merely saying that the "lack" is the gap between the physical body of Christ on earth as the first century man—Jesus of Nazareth, and His eternal, universal body—the church. Therefore, Paul is able to *rejoice* that his suffering is not in vain, but rather has become the growing pains of a church body that is maturing and becoming stronger.

Because of the unlimited potential you have within you to bring compassion to a broken world, don't make too much of your suffering or dwell on it too long. Don't withdraw from the world today but, engage it. Individualists will become active agents of redemption in the world if they don't allow themselves to get

---

2   "Saints Perpetua and Felicity," Franciscan Media, March 7, 2021, https://www.franciscanmedia.org/saint-of-the-day/saints-perpetua-and-felicity.

3   *Apologeticus*, 50, s. 13.

4   Col. 1:24

stuck in their suffering. Pain offers perspective and empathy—but only if we allow it to turn our eyes and hearts outward. Riso and Hudson point out that Fours who take action "can be among the most life-enhancing of the personality types, bringing good out of evil, hope from hopelessness, meaning from absurdity, and saving what appeared to be lost."[5]

The Good News for Individualists is that your suffering is not the final chapter. Just as Joseph's greatest achievement and Jesus' greatest triumph followed their suffering, whatever you've experienced is not the end of your story. The grievous things done to you have not made you broken beyond repair or held you back in any way. God foreknew what you would suffer and has already made arrangements to use you, like Joseph, to impact more lives than you can imagine. Quiet your heart for a moment and listen to your pain. What is it telling you? Where is it guiding you? Is it to your neighbor, whom before you may have not offered a second thought? Is it to the refugee, those who may be without life's basic comforts we all take for granted? What about the sick, those in prison, victims of abuse, foster kids, or divorcees? Allow your past suffering to show you where you ought to go next, and listen to it closely.

→ Pray

Father, I praise You for being the God who redeems and buys back precious lost time. Because You have saved me from my troubles, I will boast about Your deliverance so others may trust in the perfect Rescuer. Break my heart for what breaks Yours. Though I don't have all the answers for the surrounding darkness, I'm thankful for the presence and guidance of the Light.

---

5   Riso and Hudson, *Personality Types*, 143.

Day 30 Reflections:

What has Jesus' suffering inspired and instilled in you?

_____

_____

_____

_____

How have you allowed your suffering to cultivate empathy toward those around you?

_____

_____

_____

What breaks your heart in the world? What divine purpose might that pain be pointing you to?

_____

_____

_____

_____

→ Respond

Write a story about a time in your past when you overcame a tough challenge with God's help and how it positively influenced others.

Day 31:

One Body, Unique Parts

If the whole body were an eye, where would be the sense of hearing? If the whole

body were an ear, where would be the sense of smell? But as it is, God arranged

the members in the body, each one of them, as he chose. If all were a single

member, where would the body be? As it is, there are many parts, yet one body.

—1 Corinthians 12:17-20

INDIVIDUALIZATION IS MY TOP STRENGTH ON THE *Clifton StrengthsFinder* assessment. It might be one of your Top 5 Strengths too! According to Gallup, having this strength means you see each person as one-of-a-kind and have a knack for seeing people's hidden talents; you are intrigued by the unique qualities others possess and try to creatively draw them out.[2] Discovering our *uniqueness* is a powerful strength.

> He who can no longer listen to his brother will soon be no longer listening to God either.
>
> –Dietrich Bonhoeffer[1]

---

1 Stephen J. Nichols, *Bonhoeffer on the Christian Life: From the Cross, for the World* (United States: Crossway, 2013), 72.

2 "What Is the Definition of Individualization?," Gallup, accessed May 14, 2021, https://www.gallup.com/cliftonstrengths/en/252272/individualization-theme.aspx.

In his well-known "body" metaphor, the apostle Paul doesn't choose *uniqueness* or *sameness*, but rather combines them together in perfect harmony. Just as the human body is to us the apex of God's creation—a marvelous machine of interconnected parts and systems working in concert to uphold a person as they walk through life—the body of Christ is both one and made up of many unique parts.

First, we must value the *uniqueness* of every part. Though it's absolutely true that we need to depend on others, a healthy body requires that every part fulfill its own unique role. The ear cannot depend on the eye to do the job of hearing nor can the eye depend on the ear to do its seeing. That's why discovering your unique role in the body matters. *Healthy unity* depends upon *healthy uniquity*.

> Without you, we would be less sensitive to the pain and beauty around us and unable to know what to do with it.

I believe the perfect bodily metaphor for the Four's unique contribution to the church is the nervous system. Much like the sensory neurons in our nervous system, Fours feel things in their environment before everyone else, which sometimes can lead to feeling overwhelmed by all the emotional data flying in. But once they've taken time to process these messages, they can step into the gap with words and creative works. Like the motor neurons, Fours communicate feelings to the body of Christ in such a way that it causes a reaction: our hands lifted, feet walking, and mouths singing. Without you, we would be less sensitive to the pain and beauty around us and unable to know what to do with it.

Second, we must also value each unique part *equally*. Paul makes a big deal about this when he explains, "If the whole body were an eye, where would be the sense of hearing? If the whole body were an ear, where would be the sense of smell?"[3] Paul goes even further by calling us to "bestow the greater honor" to those who have more "ordinary" gifts and calls those who stand out more to have greater humility.[4] Rather than believing their vital roles set them above the community, healthy Fours are able to communicate our equality through their sense of our unique offerings.

---

3   1 Cor. 12:17

4   1 Cor. 12:23

Jessica Kantrowitz encourages us to see our entire Christian community as a network of lifelines rather than putting substantial weight on just one person: "I know I can vent about chronic illness to Matteo and he will understand, or text Gina and she will immediately pray for me. I can message Susi and she will be ready to offer her limited free time for a lunch date, or I can express my frustrations about misogyny to Laura or Fen, and they will respond with empathy and readiness to fight on my behalf. In other words, I've built a team."[5]

The Good News for Individualists is that Christ holds all of us together.[6] We have a good head on our shoulders. As Paul says, "Speaking the truth in love, we are to grow up in every way into him who is the head, into Christ, from whom the whole body, joined and held together by every joint with which it is equipped, when each part is working properly, makes the body grow so that it builds itself up in love."[7]

When a you are healthy, you will admire the other parts of the body rather than envying their contributions. You will depend on others and allow them to give you reality checks when your feelings drag you down or carry you away. Rather than being repelled by your *sameness* with others, you will use your commonalities to connect fully in the present, "drawing people around the cozy fire of your own spirit."[8]

→ Pray

Father, the intricate design of our human bodies points us to ascribe praise to a wonderful Creator. Thank You for arranging Your church in the same way. Forgive me of my self-importance that often puts up walls with others. Thanks be to Jesus for tearing down those walls on the cross and uniting all things. Fill me with the Spirit to work in beautiful harmony with others.

---

5   Kantrowitz, *The Long Night*, 94-95.

6   Col. 1:17

7   Eph. 4:15-16

8   Kantrowitz, *The Long Night*, 156.

Day 31 Reflections:

How does a better understanding of your gifting provide guidance on what you should be doing?

What are some ways an individualistic mindset has negatively affected our culture and churches? How does the gospel challenge that mindset and create a better way?

How will you seek to encourage, strengthen, and bestow honor to the more ordinary, less visible members of the body of Christ?

→ Respond

Name the people who are potential lifelines and how they can support you in different areas. Additionally, find an online support group that may be able to help you with one of your struggles.

Day 32:

The Theater of the Gospel

Husbands, love your wives, as Christ loved the church and gave himself up for her, that he might sanctify her, having cleansed her by the washing of water with the word, so that he might present the church to himself in splendor, without spot or wrinkle or any such thing, that she might be holy and without blemish.

—Ephesians 5:25-27

On Sundays, our church buildings fill their stages with preachers and musicians, but on Mondays, Kevin Vanhoozer says, "The church is a company of players gathered together to stage scenes of the kingdom of God for the sake of a watching world." He adds that this "theater of the gospel" is "the place where the reconciliation achieved by the cross is to be played out in scenes large and small."[2] In many ways, Sunday mornings are simply a *practice*

> The church is the theater of the gospel.
>
> —Kevin J. Vanhoozer[1]

1   Kevin J. Vanhoozer, *The Drama of Doctrine: A Canonical-Linguistic Approach to Christian Theology* (Louisville: Presbyterian Publishing Corporation, 2005), 413.

2   Ibid, 32.

and *reminder*: a weekly anchor point for what ought to be our posture toward the *whole* world, *every* day.

Made in the image of God, we take our cues from the Divine Choreographer, imitating the dance of heaven. Seventh century theologian, John of Damascus, likened the Triune God to a "circle dance."[3] Similarly, theologian Shirley Guthrie emphasizes the relational aspect of the dance: "The oneness of God is not the oneness of a distinct, self-contained individual; it is the unity of a community of persons who love each other and live together in harmony."[4]

While this vision of the divine community might be inspiring to you—a refreshing view of God and of what God's church could be—you may also find yourself disillusioned that the local church does not even come close to meeting that ideal. On one hand, you have every right to feel disillusioned: we live in a megachurch culture intent on marketing itself, following the precepts of corporate and political luminaries rather than those of the poor, itinerant Rabbi whose name we bear. It can be easy to lose faith in a spiritual climate where pastors maintain

> Jesus is extending an invitation to you today to fall head-over-heels in love with His bride—warts and all!

their own online personas and brands, where leaders nakedly pursue and protect power, where women are silenced, the disabled are forgotten, and people of color are covertly (and sometimes overtly) discriminated against. Today's church often feels anything *but* authentic—which is, of course, the aspect of community for which Fours most deeply long.

However, we must remember that, though genuineness may be a hallmark of our lives, that does not translate to perfect. The famous nineteenth century preacher Charles Spurgeon speaks directly to the heart of a disillusioned son and daughter of Christ: "If I had never joined a church until I had found one that was perfect, I should never have joined one at all; and the moment I did join it, if I had found

---

3 *Perichoresis*, in which each member is linked to all the others, offering and receiving momentum simultaneously.

4 George Cladis, *Leading the Team-Based Church: How Pastors and Church Staffs Can Grow Together into a Powerful Fellowship of Leaders* (United States: Wiley, 1999), 92.

one, I would have spoiled it, for it would not have been a perfect church after I had become a member of it."[5]

If you can hold onto Christ in all of this and have the courage to enter the dance, you will immediately add depth, beauty, and much-needed perspective for all. Richard Rohr teaches, "In the church [Fours] are advocates and designers of creative services. They have a sense of liturgy, ritual, and shaping space."[6] Rohr adds that Fours equip the church to engage the *whole* world with the *wholeness* of Christ: "Fours are by nature ecumenically oriented. They reject the division of the world into 'sacred' and 'profane.'"[7] Practically-speaking, your sense of the grey space between what is typically considered "holy" and what is considered "secular" will prophetically speak out against *dualism*—the view that some subjects, schools, careers, and callings are more "spiritual" than than others. This dualism makes the bringing of Christ's "salt and light" presence into every sphere of culture totally impossible.

The Good News for Individualists is though the local church is far less than ideal in its current state, Jesus is faithful to His beloved bride. Paul mentions to the Ephesian church that "Christ loved the church and gave himself up for her."[8] Right now, in the unseen world behind a curtain, Jesus is faithfully working to "present the church to himself in splendor, without spot or wrinkle or any such thing, that she might be holy and without blemish."[9] Jesus is extending an invitation to you today to fall head-over-heels in love with His bride—warts and all! Rather than withdraw from, criticize, or tarnish the church, would you participate with Jesus in His work to beautify her? Would you let yourself be drawn into the Trinitarian dance of giving yourself away to love, support, and honor others?

---

5   Charles Spurgeon, "2234. The Best Donation," Answers in Genesis, Sermon delivered on April 5, 1891, https://answersingenesis.org/education/spurgeon-sermons/2234-the-best-donation/.

6   Rohr and Ebert, *The Enneagram*, 100.

7   Ibid, 98.

8   Eph. 5:25

9   Eph. 5:27

Day 32 Reflections:

If you could dream up the ideal church, what would it look like?

_____

_____

_____

_____

Where have you been disillusioned with the local and global church?

_____

_____

_____

_____

What attitudes or actions will you change in light of Jesus' scandalous commitment to His imperfect bride?

_____

_____

_____

_____

→ **Respond**

If you've been absent from a church community, go find one and enter the dance, as awkward as it might feel.

Day 33:

Thick Skin, Soft Heart

Be kind to one another, tenderhearted, forgiving one another, as God in Christ

forgave you.

—Ephesians 4:32

SOME PEOPLE SEEM TO HAVE BEEN BORN with a thick skin, able to take pushback, side-glances, or even insults in stride; and sometimes, they don't even notice such things have occurred. Many of us, however, have to work overtime to overcome such sleights—real or perceived. This work is necessary to experience

> When you are immune to the opinions and actions of others, you won't be the victim of needless suffering.
>
> –Miguel Ruiz[1]

longevity in relationships and our vocations. For better and worse, Fours are constantly picking up signals from the outside world. Often this leads to intuitive understanding of other people's struggles, joys, and pains; however, they are also constantly receiving information on whether they are accepted or validated—a negative facial expression, body

---

1 Don Miguel Ruiz, *The Four Agreements: A Practical Guide to Personal Freedom* (United States: Amber-Allen, 2011), 50.

movement, or extended silence might be all that it takes to induce a tailspin of inadequacy and shame.

One thing that personally resonated with me is Fours' tendency to anticipate rejection. I often feel this struggle in my own heart, automatically assuming that others are going to reject me based on a series of intangible signals they may

> Being tender is more powerful than being tough.

not have meant to send, or that may not even be an accurate representation of their thoughts. One humorous story illustrates how this tendency can become a self-fulfilling prophecy:

> "Someone goes round to a friend's place to ask if he can borrow the friend's guitar. On the way there, as he approaches the house, it occurs to him that it is a bad time to visit, since his friend might be having lunch. A few minutes later, still on the way there, he imagines that not only will he bother his friend, but that his friend will not be very willing to lend him his guitar. A guitar is a very personal thing for someone who spends so much of his time playing it. He knocks on the door and when his friend opens it with a smile and asks after the motive of his visit, the other person can do no more than reply: 'You and your guitar can go to hell!'"[2]

I laughed out loud when I read that! If you ever start to feel this way too, remember the adage that "feelings aren't facts"—yet we should not utterly ignore them. Feelings flowing from your old self or experiences may cause you to overinterpret or overread every facial expression or comment people make, attributing shades to thoughts on which we have no accurate information. We don't live in others' heads, but the more we try, the more likely they end up living in ours.

One helpful practice is to ask others more often to clarify what they mean—and then to simply trust they are telling the truth. Another helpful practice is to reframe constructive criticism as an opportunity for growth. When people care enough about us—our lives and our work—to offer feedback in a spirit of loving support, we owe it to them to get past our hurt feelings or any violated sense of artistic expression and consider their words. Lastly, ignore the people on the

---

2 Naranjo, *The Enneagram of Society*, 126-127.

sidelines. Don't give the time of day to the social media trolls, basement bloggers, body-shamers, ministry critics, or anyone else who hasn't earned your trust!

The Good News for Individualists is that it's possible to have a thick skin and retain a soft heart—to be sensitive to ours and others' feelings, while also allowing them to be merely the weather surrounding the mountain of our identity in Christ. Jesus embodied this by displaying a sensitivity toward the feelings, needs, and hurts of the "lost sheep of the house of Israel,"[3] while at the same time not allowing the sheep's enthusiasm for Him—or the scheming of the religious wolves—to push Him off course.

Though your sensitivity may not be embraced as a strength where you work or live, know that your soft heart is a beautiful reflection of the *imago Dei*. You illustrate beautifully God's call for every Christian to be tender-hearted[4] and sympathetic.[5] This is why your leadership and participation in the community matters. Keep engaging the hurt, depressed, wounded, and underdogs of the world, showing us that being tender is more powerful than being tough.

→ Pray

Father, forgive me for the ways I've been overly sensitive and too reactionary to the myriad of signals I receive every day. Hold me steady so that I can withstand the thoughtlessness of insensitive people and the baseless fears of those who mean me no harm. Don't let me throw in the towel or give up too quickly on my relationships; help me to see that these present trials are building greater endurance within me so I can be used in even greater ways in the decades to come.

---

3   Matt. 15:24

4   Eph. 4:32

5   1 Pet. 3:8

Day 33 Reflections:

Do you see your sensitivity as a God-given strength or liability? How have others affirmed your tender heart?

_____

_____

_____

_____

What is the most insensitive thing someone could say or do to you?

_____

_____

_____

_____

How were others insensitive toward Jesus? How does Jesus' response and leaning into the Father teach you to respond to others' insensitivity toward you?

_____

_____

_____

_____

→ Respond

Part of being tender and sensitive toward others means we use active listening skills. To do this, listen intently as someone shares with you, then summarize and reflect back to them what you think you heard to check for accuracy. This helps you avoid jumping to conclusions and to gain an accurate understanding.

Day 34:

Outside the Box

When the donkey saw the angel of the LORD, she lay down under Balaam. And Balaam's anger was kindled, and he struck the donkey with his staff. Then the LORD opened the mouth of the donkey, and she said to Balaam, "What have I done to you, that you have struck me these three times?"

—Numbers 22:27-28

I see a lot of big issues facing the church today, but I think most of them result in one way or another from an impoverished imagination.

–Karen Swallow[1]

THE TALKING DONKEY IS ONE OF THE most unforgettable stories in the Bible. Balaam saddles his donkey and sets out on a journey. On his way, God sends an angel to block Balaam's progress. Three different times the donkey refuses to keep going, and all three times Balaam strikes his donkey. After the beast could endure no more, it turned its head and miraculously says, "What have I done to you ... Am I not your donkey, on

---

1   Beth Felker Jones, "Enriching Our Imagination: An Interview with Karen Swallow Prior," Firebrand Magazine, January 18, 2021, https://firebrandmag.com/articles/enriching-our-imagination-an-interview-with-karen-swallow-prior.

which you have ridden all your life long to this day?"[2] I wish I could have seen Balaam's face.

Aside from the theological lesson and humor in this story, why did God choose a talking donkey? And while we are on the topic, why did God tell Isaiah to strip off his clothes and wander around naked for three years?[3] Why did God tell Jeremiah to bury his newly purchased underwear in a rock or Ezekiel to eat a scroll?[4] Why did God visit Mary with such a strange promise of pregnancy?[5] Why were *these* things His chosen method?

The simple but profound answer to that question is this: *to grab our attention.*

Thankfully, the Bible is not nearly as boring as many of our churches—our faith has a long history of poetic preachers, songwriters, and storytellers whom God uses to put on a public performance to wake us up. In fact, one-third of the Old Testament is poetry, and Jesus Himself used illustrative parables instead of three-point sermons to grab our attention. Are Chritians today full of wonder and intrigue, or are we flat and predictable?

> When current methods are not working, we need someone to step up and transpose the well-worn sheet music of life into another key.

Jacob LaValle, a Nashville artist, was recently asked in an online interview, "What rules (in making music) need to be broken?" He responded, "I think any rules which stand in the way of the communication of a certain sought after feeling are the ones that need to be broken ... When the set of current rules, or toolbox, is lacking in its ability to communicate a feeling effectively, new things will begin to be created out of necessity."[6] That insight is profound for both music and faith. When current methods are not working, we need someone to step up

---

2   Num. 22:28,30

3   Isa. 20

4   Jer. 13; Ezek. 3

5   Luke 1:30-31

6   "Behind the piano: Jacob LaValle," Sleepy Songs, October 24, 2019, https://sleepysongs.se/behind-the-piano/behind-the-piano-jacob-lavalle/.

and transpose the well-worn sheet music of life into another key—arousing the curiosity of sincere seekers and hearts of complacent believers.

I want to personally challenge you today to continue questioning the status quo. One of your great gifts to the world is an ability to see into life's greys, to feel the constant need to question everything. There are too many people who are content with the way things are, going directly against God's command in Genesis to create and cultivate.[7] Use your passion for excellence to help your ministry or workplace take a different approach even if it will take more time and money.

Additionally, encourage everyone around you to "read outside the box." Karen Swallow, a Research Professor of English and Christianity and Culture, said that the solution to our culture's "impoverished imagination" is to read more literary fiction which cognitive science has proven has the power to cultivate empathy toward people with different views or opposing sides.[8] In other words, fiction reading is a much-overlooked strategy that could help us overcome the insensitive, polarizing reality that exists in our pluralistic society today.

The Good News for Individualists is God encourages us to live outside the box, to fearlessly push our community toward uncharted waters where only doubt and loving trust can guide. We worship a God who says, "For my thoughts are not your thoughts, neither are your ways my ways."[9] Be the most reliable translation of those unknowable thoughts as you can, allowing the infinite to burst through your finitude. As you use your gifts to grab the attention of others, be careful you don't unintentionally "photobomb" Jesus. It's not hard to jump into everyone's field of view and take the credit Jesus alone deserves. When we're making a positive impact in this world, it's not because our tailored image is front and center, but because the *imago Dei* is shining through.

---

7   Gen. 2:15

8   Beth Felker Jones, "Enriching Our Imagination: An Interview with Karen Swallow Prior," Firebrand Magazine, January 18, 2021, https://firebrandmag.com/articles/enriching-our-imagination-an-interview-with-karen-swallow-prior.

9   Isa. 55:8

> **→ Pray**
>
> Father, You are profoundly creative and are always working in ways that are beyond our comprehension. Help me to see that I've been given the gift of imagination to problem-solve and wake people up from spiritual slumber. Give me courage today to confront the Balaams around me with the truth in unordinary and unconventional ways.

Day 34 Reflections:

When was the last time you said or did something that was "out of the box?"

_____

_____

_____

_____

What do you enjoy about being novel and unconventional? What's challenging?

_____

_____

_____

_____

What beautiful truths do you feel are not getting across to this generation? What can you do to get the message across in a way that grabs people's attention?

_____

_____

_____

_____

> **→ Respond**
>
> Read a novel in an unfamiliar genre.

Day 35:

Lights, Camera, Action!

Go to the ant, O sluggard; consider her ways, and be wise. Without having any

chief, officer, or ruler, she prepares her bread in summer and gathers her food

in harvest. How long will you lie there, O sluggard? When will you arise from

your sleep? A little sleep, a little slumber, a little folding of the hands to rest, and

poverty will come upon you like a robber, and want like an armed man.

—Proverbs 6:6-11

"LIGHTS, CAMERA, ACTION!" IS THE TRADITIONAL CUE to a film crew at the beginning of a take. All of the hard work —script writing, acting classes, hair and make-up, rehearsing lines—all comes down to that one climactic moment when

> Big wins are usually a collection of very small steps.
>
> –Henry Cloud[1]

the director says "Action!" Without the *action*, all of the combined creativity is in vain!

What have you been dreaming about, but haven't started yet? Fours are tremendously gifted at seeing what does not yet exist, crafting a beautiful

---

1   Henry Cloud, *9 Things You Simply Must Do to Succeed in Love and Life: a Psychologist Probes the Mystery of Why Some Lives Really Work and Others Don't* (Nashville, TN: Thomas Nelson, 2006), 84.

image of the world that could be. One of the most difficult aspects of any project—especially for Fours—is turning their idealistic dreams into reality. Jim Collins, in his bestselling book *Good to Great,* describes six things that separate good companies from great ones. One of his distinctions is called *The Flywheel Effect*:

> Picture a huge, heavy flywheel—a massive metal disk mounted horizontally on an axle, about 30 feet in diameter, 2 feet thick, and weighing about 5,000 pounds. Now imagine that your task is to get the flywheel rotating on the axle as fast and long as possible. Pushing with great effort, you get the flywheel to inch forward, moving almost imperceptibly at first. You keep pushing and, after two or three hours of persistent effort, you get the flywheel to complete one entire turn. You keep pushing, and the flywheel begins to move a bit faster, and with continued great effort, you move it around a second rotation. ... Then, at some point—breakthrough! The momentum of the thing kicks in in your favor, hurling the flywheel forward, turn after turn ... whoosh! ... its own heavy weight working for you. You're pushing no harder than during the first rotation, but the flywheel goes faster and faster.[2]

Collins uses this metaphor to point out that great companies' success comes from a series of small efforts rather than one "magic push." An ancient version of the flywheel metaphor

Talent is insufficient for success.

is the hardworking ant found in Proverbs. Do you want to get that degree, sell your art, start a business or practice, or get started on that new creative project? Just look down and "consider the ant,"[3] as Scripture suggests. The ant works tirelessly, and through slow, small movements, stores up what it needs to last through the winter.

Likewise, the Individualist will benefit from learning how to take actionable steps. The biggest challenge for Fours comes when they believe that working through all their feelings is a prerequisite to moving forward. Rather, they must "move

---

2   "The Flywheel Effect," Jim Collins - Concepts - The Flywheel Effect, accessed November 16, 2020, https://www.jimcollins.com/concepts/the-flywheel.html.

3   Prov. 6:6-8

from the world of subjectivity to the world of objectivity, from self-absorption to principled action" and begin "acting on principles rather than moods."[4]

All Enneagram types shade toward other numbers, depending on whether they are moving toward or away from health and wholeness. When the Four follows their growth path to Type One[5] they will move out of their feelings and become doers who are clear and assertive about what they want—they are structured and self-disciplined. A healthy One wakes up every day believing they are to some extent in control of their environment, so they focus more on solutions rather than dwelling on problems.

You don't have to wait for more inspiration; you just need to act on it. The first thing you can do is set up a routine that will help you accomplish one small task at a time: Look to the ant! Next, begin networking with others: talent is insufficient for success. You need like-minded people who can push you and be advocates for your dreams and gifts. Believe in yourself! A Four can easily get sucked into false narratives and give up too quickly. Remember, the first few pushes of the flywheel are always the hardest, but once you get going, you will become unstoppable.

The Good News for Individualists is that God provides the power for us to "run with endurance the race that is set before us"[6] by fixing our eyes on Jesus, who *persevered* on our behalf. Furthermore, Paul tells the Galatian church, "And let us not grow weary of doing good, for in due season we will reap, if we do not give up."[7] Remember, God measures success by our *faithfulness*, not results. We execute the small, daily steps of planting and watering, but in the end, we will say it is "God who gives the growth."[8]

---

4   Riso and Hudson, *Personality Types*, 166.

5   Enneagram theory states that in security, Fours will "step up" to the high side of Type One and in stress will "step down" to the low side of Type Two.

6   Heb. 12:1-2

7   Gal. 6:9

8   1 Cor. 3:5-7

→ Pray

Father, forgetting what lies behind and straining forward to what lies ahead, I will press on toward the goal of fulfilling my calling in Christ Jesus. Forgive me for too often withdrawing when I should be engaging the work to which You've called me. I receive Your forgiveness today and ask that You help me run my race with endurance.

Day 35 Reflections:

How have you observed your inward focus affecting your ability to take action?

When have you seen the flywheel effect playing out in your life? What lessons can you learn from your past successes?

Who can you recruit to help you "push" through the initial resistance of beginning a project?

→ Respond

Big successes start with small steps. Start a 10-minute daily workout. Set a goal to pay off a set amount of debt this month. Make a call to a counselor. Devote 10 minutes toward cleaning a different room each day this week. Moving one grain of sand every day gets the flywheel going.

Day 36:

Authentically You

But when I saw that their conduct was not in step with the truth of the gospel, I

said to Cephas before them all, "If you, though a Jew, live like a Gentile and not

like a Jew, how can you force the Gentiles to live like Jews?"

—Galatians 2:14a

I AM AN ACHIEVER, A TYPE THREE on the Enneagram. One big difference between our personality types is that Fours seek to be authentic while Threes become chameleons who shapeshift into whatever the room needs them to be. Because of this gift, I have been invited into leadership roles and even won homecoming king. The downside? I catch myself wearing multiple masks in different settings and am still trying to figure out who I really am. As artist Ryan O'Neal from Sleeping At Last sings, "It's so exhausting on this silver screen where I play the role of anyone but me."[2]

> I've always done whatever I want and always been exactly who I am.
>
> —Billie Eilish[1]

1   August Brown, "Fast-rising artist Billie Eilish shows pop's future has arrived," LA Times, March 7, 2018, https://www.latimes.com/entertainment/music/la-et-ms-billie-eilish-20180301-story.html.

2   Ryan Neal, "Sleeping At Last," Sleeping At Last, 2016, http://sleepingatlast.com.

In his letter to the Galatians, the apostle Paul recalls a time he called out Peter for wearing multiple masks. While in Antioch, Peter gave the Gentiles the impression he was comfortable eating with them, which was—as it still is—a sign of acceptance and extension of community. However, when the more orthodox Jewish-Christian leaders showed up from Jerusalem, Peter feared the reaction of his countrymen and distanced himself from the new Gentile converts, creating a rift in the fledgling community. Paul—who had worked so hard to bring these groups together—publicly called out this duplicitous behavior, reminding Peter that such hypocrisy was out of step with the gospel.

The word *hypocrite* is an ancient Greek theater term that Jesus, in particular, turned on the two-faced religious leaders of His day. Whereas authenticity is about being honest, vulnerable, and truthful, hypocrites are always playing a part, hiding behind the words or actions they think are acceptable to their audience. Everything in today's world—from our highly polarized, performative politics, to the daily draw to present a perfect image on social media—seems to add layers of hypocrisy and falsehood upon reality. I've witnessed the shift over the past few decades toward distrusting church leaders who are formal, inauthentic, or too black and white. Church members are fed up with all the masks and the unsustainable holiness codes, and are starving for raw connections.

> You have an opportunity to help the Western church shed its shiny veneer before it's too late.

Your gift of authenticity has never been in demand more than it is right now. The world is longing to see Christ followers who are vulnerable about their mental health, forthcoming about their doubts or disillusionment, truthful about what they really want, and willing to talk about the topics no one else wants to address. You have an opportunity to help the Western church shed its shiny veneer before it's too late.

I envy you, and I'm taking notes. I love the way you invite God and others to look within your heart, bravely shining light on the dark corners most of us try to ignore or hide. You embody David's song perfectly: "Search me, O God, and know my heart! Try me and know my thoughts! And see if there be any grievous way in me, and lead me in the way everlasting!"[3] You inspire me not to imitate other preachers, but to find my own voice, giving me the courage to ask the question, "Who am *I*?" rather than "Who do they want me to be?" I've seen your passion, the criticism you've received for it, and desperately want to say, "Well done, sister. Well done, brother."

In this struggle, remember to take authenticity all the way. Authenticity is not simply acknowledging your brokenness but learning to live well through it. Paul exhorts you "to put off your old self ... and to put on the new self, created after the likeness of God in true righteousness and holiness."[4] Let your Christian ministry be such that it not only invites people into authentic fellowship, but also encourages them to grow into wholeness through vulnerably sharing.

The Good News for Individualists is that God created you to be your redeemed self and no one else. You don't have to apologize for "I am" statements because you are a reflection of the great "I AM," with whom "there is no variation or shadow due to change."[5] You were not created to be a prisoner to the expectations of others. You are loved for who you are, not for who others want you to be, and love, when perfected, casts out fear[6]—fear of the judgment of God or humans.

→ Pray

Father, I'm thankful that You enjoy searching the depths of my heart. You are the One who is most aware of the darkest parts of me, and yet, You have lavished Your love on me through Christ. If there is anything grievous within me, please show me. If there is anything I'm still hiding behind, please take it away. I want to live fully transparent before You, and show others how to do the same.

---

3   Ps. 139:23-24

4   Eph. 4:22-24

5   Jas. 1:17

6   1 John 4:18

Day 36 Reflections:

How have you seen God use your vulnerability to affect other people in a deep way?

_____

_____

_____

_____

How do you sometimes use a lower level of authenticity as "fig leaves" to hide behind?

_____

_____

_____

_____

Where do you see inauthenticity around you? What does it look like to lead with the gift of authenticity?

_____

_____

_____

_____

➜ Respond

Pick three to four people you trust—family, friends, or coworkers. Ask each one of them, separately, to list three strengths they think you have and send them to you. Then, compile all the strengths: make a picture, list, or chart to represent their responses. Use this as an encouragement on the tough days to remind you that you are seen and loved for who you are.

Day 37:

Compassionate Parenting

Hear, O Israel: The LORD our God, the LORD is one. You shall love the LORD your God with all your heart and with all your soul and with all your might. And these words that I command you today shall be on your heart. You shall teach them diligently to your children, and shall talk of them when you sit in your house, and when you walk by the way, and when you lie down, and when you rise.

—Deuteronomy 6:4-7

To be in your children's memories tomorrow, you have to be in their lives today.

–Barbara Johnson[1]

THE INDIVIDUALIST'S NATIVE GIFTS OFFER THE OPPORTUNITY to be an incredible parent, caregiver, and mentor. When moving toward health, they can leave a lasting imprint of expansive love on those under their influence. As Jacqui Pollock, author of *Knowing Me Knowing Them*, explains,

---

1 Barbara Johnson, *The Best Devotions of Barbara Johnson* (United States: Zondervan, 2010), 109.

Day 37

Your creative mind expands your children's horizons and allows them to think expansively. Your deep sense of empathy allows you to show compassion for your children. You are in tune with feelings and you encourage your children to get in touch with theirs—they feel understood and a deep sense of connection. You are intuitive and have a sense of what's going on for your children—you have a deep appreciation of their world. You encourage an appreciation of beauty, refinement, elegance and uniqueness that develops your children's appreciation of the finer things in life.[2]

This beautiful vision of a child growing up knowing they are seen and understood on a deep level—and challenged to seek the depths of life—is what most of us hope our loved ones receive. However, we are not always moving toward health. While every parent will fail many times in their attempts to steward the

> When you confidently walk in God's acceptance, you will exude belovedness.

lives they've been charged with, there are unique ways a Four—particularly one in stress—can negatively affect those they love. Pollock points out three areas a Four should be on guard for that may lead to unwanted outcomes.

First, a Four's tendency to notice what's lacking in the world, if consistently projected on a child, may lead them to grow with a sense of inadequacy. Second, a Four's occasional moodiness and oversensitivity may cause anxiety in the home, draining the family's emotional energy. And lastly, relational disconnection may happen when a Four feels alienated, unworthy, jealous, or hurt—all feelings a still-growing child may engender as they lash out—and then outwardly parades their resentment. Loved ones may then find it extremely difficult to show love and compassion after the Four has withdrawn and completely shut down.[3]

As we look to the Bible, we find King David thriving as a military and political leader, but struggling as a father. Amnon, Absalom, Adonijah, and Solomon go on to worship idols, gather a harem of lovers, and do unspeakable things. However,

---

2 Jacqui Pollock, Margaret Loftus and Tracy Tresidder, *Knowing Me, Knowing Them: Understand Your Parenting Personality by Discovering the Enneagram* (Australia: Monterey Press, 2014), 88.

3 Ibid, 89-91.

as we look to the New Testament, Eunice—mother to the apostle Paul's protege, Timothy—offers a vastly different legacy as a parent. Eunice is present in her son, Timothy's, life and teaches him about Jesus so that her son's heart is prepared to receive the message and burden Paul brings. In her turn, she inherits a sincere faith from her mother, Lois, both of whom teach Timothy the Scriptures.[4]

In addition to the vastly important work of entrusting your faith to the children in your life, remember these strategies for growth from Pollock. First, we will only give what we ourselves have—whether that be the gift of intuitive empathy, an expansive imagination, and thirst for plumbing life's depths, or crippling insecurity and emotional inconsistency. When you confidently walk in God's acceptance, you will exude belovedness. Offer this same implacable acceptance to your children. Second, enjoy the ordinary things in the day, and use your talent for finding beauty in the mundane in your loved ones' lives. Third, learn how to set boundaries. Your desire to have meaningful connections with your children may overwhelm them at times, so be sure you give them enough space. And lastly, rather than pausing to indulge your own emotions when they arise, remind yourself to focus on the task at hand of helping your children regulate their own internal world.[5]

The Good News for Individualists is that, though we are imperfect parents, caregivers, and mentors, God is our perfect Father whose love never ceases toward us. He's never too busy to extend the hand of loving acceptance to you, as His child, and remind you: "I'm not disappointed in you." When your emotions are strong, He doesn't get overwhelmed but seeks to draw you in closer, just as Jesus received children with open arms and rebuked the disciples who thought these little ones would be too much for Him.[6]

---

4   2 Tim. 1:5; 3:14-15

5   Pollock, *Knowing Me, Knowing Them*, 96.

6   Matt. 19:14

→ **Pray**

Father, help me to cling to the promise that if I train children up in the way they should go—in modeling a posture of wonder and acceptance—then they will not depart from it when they get old. Fill me with Your Holy Spirit so that the children around me will see the gospel of Your love in action in their own lives. Let my most significant achievement be loving and accepting others just as You have loved me.

Day 37 Reflections:

How have your unique strengths positively influenced the children in your life?

_____

_____

_____

Which strategy for growth would you like to work on improving this week?

_____

_____

_____

What opportunities are there in your home, extended family, or church community to teach and model the gospel for children or teens?

_____

_____

_____

→ **Respond**

If you are a parent, schedule a consistent weekly "date" with each of your children. Let them pick the place and activity. If you aren't a parent, look for an opportunity to come alongside a family this week and offer your support.

Day 38:

Aristocrats in Exile

Do nothing from selfish ambition or conceit, but in humility count others more

significant than yourselves.

—Philippians 2:3

AMERICA IS OFTEN CHARACTERIZED AS A THREE, or Achiever country, whereas France is the symbolic land of the Individualist. France is set apart, refined, and somewhat elitist with its long history of opulent aristocracy, high culture, and haute cuisine.[2] Fours are well known for their love of the finer things in life; they would often rather go without than have a lesser experience. It's been said they can "forgive almost anything except bad taste!"[3]

Everyone is so obsessed with themselves nowadays that they have no time for me.

–Louise Rennison, author and comedian[1]

Some Fours very well may be "prima donnas," giving off a haughty or snobbish attitude because of an inflated conception of their own originality—as one Four teenager said, "Sometimes I think I was a

1 Chestnut, *The 9 Types of Leadership*, 135.

2 Rohr and Ebert, *The Enneagram*, 108.

3 Ibid, 178.

princess mistakenly born into a family of peasants."[4] Yet much of the time, if there is an appearance of superiority, it is unintentional. Deep down, Fours are typically insecure, longing to be accepted for all their uniqueness, feeling misunderstood and painfully out of place or time. Like the nobles fleeing France during the revolution, a Four may view themself as an "Aristocrat in Exile" as Jerome Wagner puts it.[5]

Whether you appear standoffish because you are in an unhealthy place, or it's an unintentional side-effect of dwelling in your rich internal life, or simply a manifestation of social anxiety due to those feelings of otherness—it's good to be aware of this common "vibe" others receive. Remember Jesus' humble engagement with others, even when He wanted to be alone to commune with

> Our impressiveness is not tied to our status or nobility but our proximity to Jesus.

His father.[6] We ought to follow Paul's admonition based on that example: "Do nothing from selfish ambition or conceit, but in humility count others more significant than yourselves."[7] The apostle offered motivation for this selfless way of living by pointing to Christ's drilling down to the foundational definition of being human—servanthood.[8]

To live by this definition, we must first avoid *selfish ambition*: putting others' needs first. We should fearlessly jump in to serve the group, even if recognition for our work is unlikely. Depth of meaning is made in finding beauty in the everyday, especially in the service of others.

Second, avoid *conceit* by refraining from cultivating a grandiose version of yourself, leading to an inflated sense of your originality over those around you.

The opposite side to avoiding conceit and the third response is to count others as *more significant* than yourself. Nines, for instance, tend to see the world through

---

4   Elizabeth Wagele, *The Enneagram for Teens: Discover Your Personality Type and Celebrate Your True Self* (United States: PLI MEDIA, 2014).

5   Wagner, *Nine Lenses*, 279.

6   Matt. 14

7   Phil. 2:3

8   Phil. 2:6-7

the lens of everyone else, but Fours see the world primarily through their own lens. This is not an inherently negative statement: your rich inner life and populated imagination tends to fill your view almost completely—plus you desperately want to be understood and so expend a lot of mental energy thinking about how to best present yourself. It can take a lot of work to invite someone into that space. However, while seeing the world solely through others' eyes can create an almost chameleon-like existence, being self-referential may lead to a lot of "I" and "me" in your communication, causing others to perceive this as self-centered.

Lastly, live every day with the mentality that God chooses ordinary people. Jesus' disciples were not elite in any way, but were simple men and women. The impressiveness of these common people was not tied to their status or nobility, but their proximity to Jesus: "Now when they saw the boldness of Peter and John, and perceived that they were uneducated, common men, they were astonished. And they recognized that they had been with Jesus."[9]

The Good News for Individualists is that Jesus showed us the path of downward mobility and servanthood: "Though he was in the form of God, did not count equality with God a thing to be grasped, but emptied himself, by taking the form of a servant ... "[10] Jesus did not grow up around nobility which Nathanael sarcastically pointed out: "Can anything good come out of Nazareth?"[11] He took a blue collar job, washed His disciples' dirty feet, and associated with the lowly— the poor, crippled, lame, and blind.[12] Following His example, we become lowly before the noble *and* the needy, our friends *and* our enemies.

→ Pray

Father, thank You for making me so unique and special. You fashioned me in the womb with creative delight and look upon me everyday with sheer pleasure. Open my ears so that I can hear You singing over me today. Relax the impulse within me to be a "somebody" in the eyes of the world. Give me eyes to see and hands to serve those who I too often dismiss as unimportant.

---

9   Acts 4:13

10   Phil. 2:6-7

11   John 1:46

12   Luke 14:12-15

Day 38 Reflections:

What is so alluring about pursuing a "high culture" way of life?

_____

_____

_____

_____

What is striking about Jesus's decision to have an ordinary body, birthplace, occupation, and leadership team? How were His disciples able to leave a unique legacy without cultural rank or status?

_____

_____

_____

_____

How is God prompting you to count others as more significant than yourself?

_____

_____

_____

_____

➜ Respond

Go spend some time today with someone who might not be viewed as important in the eyes of the world.

Day 39:

The Secret to Contentment

Bless the LORD, O my soul, and all that is within me, bless his holy name!

Bless the LORD, O my soul, and forget not all his benefits, who forgives all your

iniquity, who heals all your diseases, who redeems your life from the pit, who

crowns you with steadfast love and mercy, who satisfies you with good so that

your youth is renewed like the eagle's.

—Psalm 103:1-5

MY FRIEND, ANTWONE'S, SOCIAL MEDIA POST CAUGHT my eye: "I am acutely focused on the negative, angering, and fearful things in the world. Help me list some things that are good about life so I can have something to hold onto other than staring into the abyss."

> The opposite of home is not distance, but forgetfulness.
>
> —Elie Wiesel[1]

What do you do when you are disillusioned with the world? We can all take a cue from my friend and reach out for help when we need to be reminded that life is still worth living, and that there is so much light bursting through

---

1 Chestnut, *The Complete Enneagram*, 57.

this often dark world. Individualists struggle with contentment because they tend to live with an overwhelming feeling that *something is missing*. This awareness can bloom into an aesthetic longing which is a forerunner to creation, or it can lead to a hyperfocus on what they *don't* have. As Leslie Hershberger says, "Fours see the best of what's missing and the worst of what is present."[2]

Do you tend to see the light at the end of the tunnel or the tunnel at the end of the light? Have you become so attached to your misfortunes that you can no longer see all the evidence of God's grace in your life? If so, then gratitude—the art of being thankful and a readiness to show appreciation to others—is the flower to tend in your life's garden.

Gratitude is cultivated through the ancient discipline of celebration—the continual remembrance of what God has and is doing in and around you. The Psalmist exhorts us to "forget not" our God who forgives, heals, redeems, crowns, and satisfies. In the same vein, Moses commanded the people of Israel, "Only take care, and keep your soul diligently, lest you forget the things that your eyes have seen, and lest they depart from your heart all the days of your life. Make them known to your children and your children's children."[3] Forgetfulness, Moses said, would be the doom of God's people (as indeed it was).[4]

> The failure to pause and reflect on our positive qualities or past successes creates a cycle of feeling like we are never enough.

When the discipline of celebration is neglected, you are training yourself to believe that what you've done isn't worthwhile. The failure to pause and reflect on our positive qualities or past successes creates a cycle of feeling like we are never enough, creating a spiral of forgetfulness for how far you have come and stealing your ability to see and celebrate the life in others.

---

2 Moser, *The Enneagram of Discernment*, 202.

3 Deut. 4:9

4 Isa. 17:10

When you accomplish something great, do you stop to acknowledge it or do you immediately move on to the next opportunity to prove yourself? When something beautiful occurs in your loved ones' lives, do you stop to point it out to them? When was the last time you created space in your busy schedule to celebrate past wins and send encouragement?

In Scripture, celebration was intentional. Miriam the prophetess picked up a tambourine and led the women in a celebration dance after the children of God were saved from the hand of Pharaoh. The Israelites recruited two choirs and rounded up the best musicians for a big party to celebrate the dedication of the wall of Jerusalem. Celebration was also pre-planned. Ancient Israel was required to gather three times every year to celebrate God and His mighty acts through festival holidays. Likewise, the traditional church has followed Israel's lead, with a calendar marking seasons and days of expectancy, celebration, and confession.[5] Therefore, don't forget to gather with your community regularly to feast, sing, and dance as a means to actively remember.

The Good News for Individualists is that you are marvelously *complete*. The secret to contentment is that we have forever-access to all of Christ's spiritual blessings, forgiveness, and righteousness. I heard Ian Cron share that he put up a note on his mirror that says, "Nothing is missing," to remind himself of that truth every day. You can let go of your imaginary, idealized secret self because you were, from conception, a creation of God's divine design. You possess an abundance of original qualities that other people (myself included) are envying right now. You are magnificent and the incredible work God is doing through you is marvelous—all you have to do today is *remember*.

→ Pray

Father, I bless Your holy name! You have forgiven my sins and redeemed my life from the pit. Your Son, Jesus, received a crown of thorns so that I would be crowned with Your steadfast love and mercy. By Your Holy Spirit, help me to never forget all You've done for me. Enable me to lead a celebratory life that rejoices in You always.

---

5 Examples: Advent is about expectancy for Christ's appearing; Christmas is the celebration of His arrival and revealing; Lent and Holy Week are the desert of testing and sharing in His passion; Easter is joy at His defeat of death with everlasting life; and Pentecost is celebrating the Holy Spirit's descent onto all creation.

Day 39 Reflections:

What are you celebrating?

_____

_____

_____

_____

How can you devote more time to the discipline of celebration?

_____

_____

_____

_____

How can you spend more time, personally or in meetings, calling out greatness in others?

_____

_____

_____

_____

➜ Respond

Start your conversations and meetings today with the question: "Where have we seen God working?"

Day 40:

Writing Your Memoir

He has made everything beautiful in its time. Also, he has put eternity into

man's heart, yet so that he cannot find out what God has done from the

beginning to the end.

—Ecclesiastes 3:11

THE AMERICAN MONK THOMAS MERTON (1915-68) HAS been referred to as the "patron saint" of Fours. His was a life of deep emotion, tragedy, and exploration of life's farthest horizons. He was born into a family of artists in France but lost both of his parents by the age of 16. He became a restless soul, traveling the world and piling up the sort of experiences that would characterize many of the Beat Generation writers who would outlive him. He moved to the US around the age of 18 and began looking into spiritual things. In 1938, he was baptized as a Catholic and pursued being a Franciscan, but was turned down after he was brutally honest about his past.

> If we want to create a different future, we must have the courage to look at the past.
>
> –Dan B. Allender

Finally, he was accepted as a candidate in 1941 at the Trappist abbey of Gethsemani, Kentucky. It was here Merton wrote his best-selling biography *The Seven Storey Mountain*. Unfortunately, his abbot thought he was taking his feelings too seriously and ordered him to stop writing for a time (though thankfully, he eventually finished his beautiful work). Merton went on to write essays against American militarism, atomic warfare, and was the target of an assasination attempt after he protested the Vietnam war.

On one visit to the hospital, Merton met a student nurse and spontaneously began a love affair. | **Will you live to tell your story?**

Being incongruent with the monastic life, he was forced to let go of his love. He traveled to the Far East and interacted with Sufi mystics, Zen Buddhists, and the Dalai Lama himself. The Dalai Lama, who had been skeptical of Christianity, grew an appreciation of it after spending time with Merton at a 1968 conference in Bangkok. Tragically and mysteriously, just a few days after this meeting, Merton was found dead in his hotel room, apparently the result of a freak, accidental electrocution. He was just 53 years old.[1]

Merton's life and writings had a profound influence on the Christian faith as it entered the second half of the twentieth century. Women and men all over the world have found freedom in his experiences, able to see a much wider spectrum of what the life of Christ can include. When Pope Francis addressed Congress in 2015, he cited Merton, along with Dorthy Day, Abraham Lincoln, and Martin Luther King Jr. as four Americans who succeeded in "seeing and interpreting reality."[2]

Have you thought about writing a memoir like Merton? Riso and Hudson explain, "Fours have a particular kind of creativity, a personal creativity, which is fundamentally autobiographical. The creativity of Fours is generally an exploration of their history and feeling world, and particularly of how their family, their loves, and various incidents from the past have affected them."[3] Fours are often the ones

---

1 This summary of Merton's story comes from Rohr and Ebert, *The Enneagram*, 113-114.

2 "The Monk Who Would Not Be Silent," Columbia College Today, accessed May 14, 2021, https://www.college.columbia.edu/cct/issue/fall18/article/monk-who-would-not-be-silent.

3 Riso and Hudson, *The Wisdom*, 201.

seeking to find expression for their journeys as a way of processing experiences. My editor (and Four), Joshua Casey just finished his memoir called *Tracking Desire: A Memoir(ish) Walk Through Faith, Failure, and Finding God Under My Feet*. If you've been swept away at all by this book, it's in large part because of his finishing touches. This is a great example of how a Four can take something ordinary and make it extraordinary!

The author of Ecclesiastes states "[God] has put eternity into man's heart."[4] This means that He has put an awareness of the future that we are all longing for into our inner being. As we labor and struggle, we must balance the very real fear that "all is vanity"[5] with the eternal hope that our inconsolable longing will one day be fulfilled.

The Good News for Individualists is that Truth became a story. John describes Jesus Christ as the incarnate *Logos*—connecting the dots for ancient esoteric thinkers by showing them that their sought-after "divine reason" became a *real* person. It's through His unordinary life, example, and path of descent— His servanthood, suffering, death, and glorious resurrection—that we find our fulfillment. After all, we are but humble, human jars of clay "to show that the surpassing power belongs to God and not to us."[6]

Will you live to tell your story? I believe you have something to say. Books like this one are helpful. (Of course, I'm pretty biased!) But sometimes, what we need more than theological points and application questions is to be swept away by divine truth getting worked out through divine beings. Your story may not give us all the answers, but it will help us to see more of this complex world through God's eyes.

Are you wondering where to sojourn next? Frederick Buechner says to go to "the place where your deep gladness and the world's deep hunger meet."[7] That's a great place to start. I'll see you there.

---

4 Eccl. 3:11

5 Eccl. 1:2

6 2 Cor. 4:7b

7 Frederick Buechner, *Wishful Thinking: A Theological ABC* (London, Mowbray, 1994), 119.

→ **Pray**

Father, I know You believe in me because I am Your beloved child, created with a purpose. Help me believe in myself. Jesus said, "If you abide in me, and my words abide in you, ask whatever you wish, and it will be done for you."[8] So I'm asking nothing less than for You to change the world through me. Use me as a main character in Your unfolding story to reconcile all things.

Day 40 Reflections:

What about Thomas Merton's life resonates with you and why?

_____

_____

_____

_____

What do you fear the most about telling the world your story? What have you buried that should be brought to light?

_____

_____

_____

How do you want the world to remember you?

_____

_____

_____

→ **Respond**

Begin writing your memoir and find a spiritual mentor to come alongside to support you in accomplishing your goals.

---

8   John 15:7

Prayer for Individualists

FATHER, I AM DEEPLY THANKFUL TO YOU for creating me uniquely in Your image with unparalleled originality. You created me to specifically reflect Your creativity and depth. I confess that too often, I long for what's missing or only see the world's shortcomings rather than showing gratitude for what's already there. Ignoring my need for belonging, I have often indulged my feelings of tortured solitude, becoming enslaved to my emotions and disengaged with ordinary life. You, being rich in empathy, saw me from heaven and sent Your Son, Jesus, to rescue me from being lost forever. Now, I revel in the fact that I belong to You and can call You my home. Clothed with the power of the Holy Spirit, I will seek to put the focus on You rather than drawing others' attention to my own unique style. Putting off envy and feelings of inferiority and superiority, and putting on my new self made in Christ's image, I will seek to steward my passion for the sake of others, inspiring beauty and excellence all around and healing the world with Christ's compassion. Amen.

Three Types of Individualists

THE THREE TYPES OF FOURS (CALLED SUBTYPES) come straight from Enneagram teacher Beatrice Chestnut, who wrote an entire book called *The Complete Enneagram* on all twenty-seven subtypes of the main nine Enneagram types.[1] As discussed in the introduction, these subtypes are helpful in drilling down the different nuances of the Individualist, which can vary so wildly that at times you may wonder how someone with *those* traits could even be the same type as you!

Before proceeding here, I offer a warning: many of these descriptions will seem overly negative. However, one of the main purposes of the Enneagram is to help us discover our "shadow self"—the ways we interact with the world unconsciously and often in times of stress. These descriptions are not indictments; rather, they are a further opportunity to deepen your awareness of how you interact with the world.

The Self-Preservation Four

These Fours are resilient and make a virtue out of endurance. They are "long-suffering"—as a way to win admiration and secure love, they are more tolerant of pain and tend to deal with misfortune more quietly than the typical Four. They may have felt growing up that it was not okay to express their needs and feelings; therefore, they internalize their envy, suffering, and shame. Although they don't communicate what's on the inside, they have the same depth and capacity for emotions as all other Fours, but instead of acknowledging or dealing with their suffering, they may become activists who try to ease the "suffering of the world" by advocating for the needy and victims of injustice. Self-Preservation Fours are called "the countertype" (which means they don't look like the typical Four) because they are more masochistic than melodramatic. They may misidentify as Sevens because they are sunny on the outside, Ones because they work hard, or Threes because they try to prove themselves. The growth path for this subtype is to acknowledge the pain and suffering on the inside, express it, and communicate their hurts and needs.

---

1   Beatrice Chestnut, *The Complete Enneagram: 27 Paths to Greater Self-Knowledge* (Berkeley, CA: She Writes Press, 2013).

The Social Four

This Four is most in touch with their emotions and so can be the most inspiring and outwardly creative. Inside, they struggle mightily to maintain a positive self-image, often wallowing in feelings of shame and inadequacy. Outwardly, however, they appear sweet, friendly, and soft. They are the most melancholy of the Fours and tend to "wear their emotions on their sleeve," attempting to secure love and engender sympathy by taking more of a victim role. This subtype struggles with comparison: they are constantly plagued by feelings of inferiority (the bottom side of comparison) but are often not willing to publicly seek attention or admiration. Rather, they long for a rescuer who will notice their suffering and come to their aid, offering validation in undying love and attention. They believe the way to happiness is through tears and that broadcasting their suffering is the shortest path to heaven—much like a child crying out to attract their parent's care and affection. This subtype tends to get stuck more often in their intense emotions and has a hard time converting them to action. Thus, the growth path for this subtype is to resist the urge to complain or stay in the role of the victim; they need to work on appreciating and speaking more highly of themselves. This subtype may look like Sixes because they tend to focus on what's missing or wrong in their lives.

The One-To-One Four

The Self-Preservation Four appears happy, the Social Four appears sad, and the One-To-One often appears mad. This Four experiences the same level of shame, deficiency, and lack as the other Fours, but externalizes their suffering in a more aggressive and impulsive way. Having a low tolerance for frustration, they complain more, demand more, and communicate their needs more directly than any other Four would dare. When the world does not see them, understand them, or acknowledge them, they become more vocal—and may even start their own revolution. Though envy drives all Fours to feel inferior, this subtype transforms envy into fuel to compete with others, overcompensating for the felt lack within; if they succeed, the feeling of superiority will allow them to come out on the top side of comparison. On the positive side, because of their natural heart-level intensity, this subtype tends to be the most present and available in relationships. The growth path for them is not to compete as much, try to complain less, and get more in touch with the fear and sadness that is at the root of the anger. This subtype may misidentify as Eights because of their anger or Twos because they can be seductive in their relationships.

Next Steps

I'M SO PROUD OF YOU FOR FINISHING this 40-day journey. That's a big accomplishment! Though this book isn't small by any means, you may feel (like me) that we've only begun to explore the tip of the iceberg. You're probably wondering: *What now? My eyes have been opened, I've grown in greater self-awareness and empathy, and now I'm ready to take the next step!* Here are some ideas:

1. Follow "Gospel for Enneagram" on Instagram, Facebook, or Twitter to continue learning and engaging.

2. Download my free resource called *Should Christians Use The Enneagram?* at gospelforenneagram.com.

3. Visit my website, gospelforenneagram.com, to find more helpful links and resources.

4. If you haven't yet, put your trust in Jesus! You can do this in your own words using the Prayer for Individualists (a few pages back) as a guide.

5. Ask a friend, spouse, or mentor to meet regularly with you to discuss the insights God has revealed to you through this book. Invite them, along with your small group, to get a devotional on their Enneagram type and share what they learn with you.

6. Join a church community where you can continue to grow in your knowledge of God and self. To go the distance, find a mentor, coach, or support system.

7. Email me with any thoughts, questions, or feedback to tyler@gospelforenneagram.com. I'd love to hear from you!

Acknowledgements

My wife: Lindsey, you show me the gospel every day by loving me for who I am and not what I do. Thank you for your tremendous encouragement to be a writer and for bearing with my workaholic tendencies. I want to be more like you.

My editors: Joshua, thank you for bringing your incredible creativity to the table. Your re-rewrites helped elevate my writing to a whole new level. Stephanie, your attention to detail and passion for this project gave me tremendous confidence. Lee Ann, your veteran experience and thoroughness increased the value of this book tremendously.

My coach: John Fooshee, thank you for your Enneagram coaching and partnership. I'm deeply grateful for your willingness to come alongside me and put wind in my sails.

My influences: I wouldn't have been able to pull this off without a multitude of direct and indirect influences such as pastors, teachers, and writers (including you, mom!) over the years. I'm deeply grateful for the spiritual heroes that have come before me and shaped me.

www.GospelForEnneagram.com

Follow us:

 /GospelForEnneagram

 @GospelForEnneagram

 @GospelForGram

Made in United States
Troutdale, OR
07/05/2024

21030665R00106